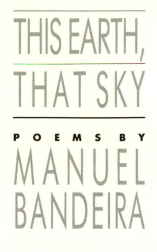

THIS EARTH,
THAT SKY

POEMS BY

MANUEL
BANDEIRA

LATIN AMERICAN LITERATURE AND CULTURE

General Editor
Roberto González Echevarría
R. Selden Rose Professor Spanish and
Professor of Comparative Literature
Yale University

1. Manuel Bandeira, *This Earth, That Sky: Poems by Manuel Bandeira,* trans. Candace Slater

THIS EARTH, THAT SKY

P O E M S   B Y

MANUEL BANDEIRA

Translated, with Notes and Introduction by
CANDACE SLATER

UNIVERSITY OF CALIFORNIA PRESS
Berkeley   Los Angeles   London

University of California Press
Berkeley and Los Angeles, California

University of California Press, Ltd.
London, England

First published by Livraria José Olympio Editora, S.A., Rio de Janeiro, Brazil.
Copyright © 1966 by Mauricio Ignácio Marcondes Souza Bandeira and Helena
Bandeira Ribeiro Cardoso.

Copyright © 1989 by The Regents of the University of California

Library of Congress Cataloging-in-Publication Data

Bandeira, Manuel, 1886–1968.
    [Estrela da vida inteira. English & Portuguese. Selections]
    This earth, that sky : poems / by Manuel Bandeira ; with English
translation, notes, and introduction by Candace Slater.
        p.   cm.
    Translation of selections from: Estrela da vida inteira.
    Includes index.
    ISBN 0-520-06090-3 (alk. paper)
    I. Title.
PQ9697.B27E8213 1989
869.1—dc19   88-20738
                                                                  CIP

Printed in the United States of America

1 2 3 4 5 6 7 8 9

For Adelaide Nielsen Slater

Contents

Preface and Acknowledgments

This book introduces the major Brazilian poet, Manuel Bandeira (1886–1968), to the English-speaking reader. Because the work of few other writers so effectively illustrates the more general problem of transition from one literary movement to another—and because the poetry itself reveals a complexity not always obvious at first glance—Bandeira deserves a wider public. The more than one hundred poems that appear here and the critical overview that serves as preface afford a comprehensive vision necessarily lacking in the handful of translations and brief critical essays available up to this point in English.[1]

The texts offered here span a half-century of writing, from the publication of his first book in 1917 to the definitive edition of his collected work in 1966. As an overwhelming majority of critics agree that Bandeira's most significant creative efforts begin in 1930 with the publication of *Libertinagem* (Libertinism), I have concentrated on this later period. The smaller number of poems drawn from Bandeira's first three books (1917, 1919, 1924) are intended to provide a basis for comparison.

The introduction that follows offers a brief summary of Bandeira's life, then examines the underlying movement of the corpus. The translator's note immediately preceding the texts considers Bandeira's poetic language in terms of the problems it poses for translation into English. The poems themselves are offered in both Portuguese and English with explanatory end notes.

Because the introduction is meant to provide an orientation for the poems that follow, I have tried to write for the reader who may know little about Brazilian poetry or Brazil. At the same time, I have sought to contribute to the existing body of Bandeira scholarship through a much-needed fresh look at the movement of his entire work. Despite the sprawling bibliography on specific aspects of Bandeira's poetry, remarkably few critics have treated the texts as a coherent whole. I have offered as a focus the poet's continuing alternation between an acceptance of, if not allegiance to, the material world and a desire for something more. It is to this fundamental—though not always obvious—opposition that the title, "This Earth, That Sky," refers.

Milton Azevedo, my colleague at the University of California at Berkeley, gave me many hours of generous assistance with these translations, and I owe him a special debt. Robert Hass and Peter Whigham made practical suggestions regarding various texts. Carlos Felipe Moisés helped me better understand Bandeira's relationship to contemporary Brazilian writing; Affonso Romano de Sant'Anna, Antônio Houaiss, and Bráulio do Nascimento clarified many details in the texts. I am grateful to Joaquim-Francisco Coelho for introducing me to Bandeira's poetry when I was a graduate student at Stanford University. In addition, I would like to express my continuing appreciation for the Fulbright, Tinker, and Guggenheim fellowships that gave me firsthand experience of Brazil and of Recife and Rio de Janeiro, which are such a vital presence in a number of Bandeira's poems.

The reactions of my students to a number of these translations were particularly useful. So were the comments of participants at both the 9th Symposium on Portuguese Traditions at the University of California, Los Angeles, and the Brazilian Literature meetings at the American Association of Teachers of Spanish and Portuguese in Madrid where draft portions of the introduction were presented. Scott Mahler and Doris Kretschmer of the University of California Press offered encouragement and counsel. My parents, Frank and Adelaide Nielsen Slater, and my husband, Paul Zingg, provided their usual welcome support.

NOTES

1. English translations of a small number of Bandeira's poems appear in *Antología de la poesía contemporanea* (*Anthology of Contemporary Latin American Poetry*), ed. Dudley Fitts (Norfolk, Conn.: New Directions, 1942), 108–123; *Modern Brazilian Poetry, An Anthology,* ed. John Nist (Bloomington: Indiana University Press, 1962), 19–29; *An Anthology of Twentieth-Century Brazilian Poetry,* ed. Elizabeth Bishop and Emanuel Brasil (Middletown, Conn.: Wesleyan University Press, 1972), 2–9; *Poesia Brasileira Moderna, A Bilingual Anthology,* ed. José Neistein and Manoel Cardozo (Washington, D.C.: Brazilian-American Cultural Institute, 1972), 46–59; *The Penguin Book of Latin American Verse,* ed. E. Caracciolo-Trepo (Middlesex: Penguin Books, 1971), 64–66; and *The Poem Itself,* ed. Stanley Brunshaw (New York: Holt, Rinehart and Winston, 1960), 194–197. Bandeira mentions an English translation of his "Mozart no Céu" (Mozart in Heaven) by Dudley Poore, but I have been unable to locate it.

Articles in English about Bandeira's poetry include Gary Bower, "Graphics, Phonics, and the 'Concrete Universal' in Manuel Bandeira's Concretist Poetry," *Luso-Brazilian Review*, III, no. 1 (1966): 19–37; David William Foster, "Manuel Bandeira's 'Poética': A Structural Approach to Its *Escritura*," *Hispania* 63 (1980): 316–320; John Nist, "Manuel Bandeira: Modern Lyric Poet of Brazil," *Arizona Quarterly* 18 (1962): 217–228; Giovanni Pontiero, "The Expression of Irony in Manuel Bandeira's *Libertinagem*," *Hispania* 48 (1962): 843–849; and C. Russell Reynolds, "The Santa Maria Egipcíaca Motif in Modern Brazilian Letters," *Romance Notes* 13 (1971): 71–76. (The latter discusses both Bandeira's "Balada de Santa Maria Egipcíaca" and Rachel de Queiroz's "A Beata Maria do Egito." See also the special issue on Bandeira, *Commemorative Series*, no. 9 (Riverside: University of California, Riverside, Latin American Studies Center, in press).

Introduction

BANDEIRA IN CONTEXT

Manuel Bandeira (1886–1968) is one of Brazil's most important poets.[1] His writing, although resolutely private in some respects, reveals an evolution that suggests far larger transformations in the nation as a whole. Born in the last years of the Brazilian Empire, when most intellectuals were still taking their cues directly from Europe, Bandeira would become a leader in the experimental, intensely nationalistic Modernist movement of the 1920s.[2] His poetry is compelling as a reflection and as a vehicle of the transition from one epoch to another.

Bandeira's family left his birthplace, the Pernambucan capital of Recife, for Rio de Janeiro when he was four years old. In 1892, they returned to Recife. Four years later, they resumed residence in Rio where Bandeira would spend most of his adult life. His relatively brief stay in Recife was essential in the formation of a powerful personal mythology. Despite long association with the urban South, he considered himself a northeasterner until the end of his life. "When I compare these four years of my childhood to any other four years of my adult life," he comments in the autobiographical *Itinerário de Pasárgada* (Itinerary of Pasárgada), "I am amazed by the emptiness of the latter in comparison to the density of that distant time."[3]

The future poet's instructors in Rio's celebrated Colégio Pedro II introduced him to the *Lusiads* and other classics as well as to the work of the best-known writers of the epoch. A chance encounter in a trolley car with Brazil's greatest nineteenth-century novelist, Machado de Assis, deeply affected the young man. During this period, he also experimented with art—particularly drawing—and music, subjects he would later write about at length.[4]

In accordance with his (engineer) father's long-standing ambitions for him, Bandeira enrolled as an architecture student in São Paulo in 1903. Before the end of the school year, however, tuberculosis struck,

1

forcing him to abandon his career plans and marking the beginning of a lifelong struggle against ill health.[5] This early awareness of mortality and experience of personal loss was largely responsible for the transformation in his vision of poetry: from pastime, or *divertimento*, to necessity (*necessidade*) and fateful destiny (*fatalidade*).

During the next few years, Bandeira underwent numerous rest cures. In 1913, he traveled to the Swiss sanatorium of Clavadel, later made famous by Thomas Mann in *The Magic Mountain*. Here he met a number of young artists, including Paul Eugène Grindel, the poet who was to be known as Paul Éluard.[6] On leaving the sanatorium, Bandeira asked his doctor how long he might expect to live. "Five, ten, fifteen years. Who knows?" was the reply. The publication of his first book of poems, *A Cinza das Horas* (Ash of the Hours), in 1917 was a defiant response to this gloomy prognosis. This work, like *Carnaval* (Carnival) and *O Ritmo Dissoluto* (Freed Rhythm), which were published in 1919 and 1924, respectively, reveals the author's bitterness at the limits imposed on him by illness.

The texts are clearly influenced by Parnassianism and Symbolism, the two principal movements in late-nineteenth-century Brazilian poetry.[7] Parnassianism, a kind of neoclassicist reaction against the more sentimental and diffuse aspects of Romanticism, began in France. *Parnasse contemporain*, the anthology that appeared in 1866, 1871, and 1876, had a marked influence on the large number of Brazilian writers accustomed to looking to Paris for inspiration. Like the Realists, their contemporaries in the field of fiction, the Parnassians sought to portray the world in dispassionate, objective terms. In line with their theory of "art for art's sake," they tried to express what they deemed to be timeless aesthetic values through carefully controlled poetic forms. Their enthusiasm for the sculptor and the jeweler produced a highly detailed, visually oriented verse.

Although the Symbolists continued the pursuit of beauty, they revealed a growing concern for the intangible. The movement's adherents relied heavily on metaphor to convey a sense of fragmentation. While they were likely to look to music, rather than the plastic arts, for models, most of these writers resembled the Parnassians in their lack of interest in social problems. Their enthusiasm for the mystic and exotic led their critics to deride them as *nefelibatas*, or cloud dwellers, who had allowed art to replace life.

Bandeira's early poems belie this Parnassian-Symbolist heritage in their preoccupation with fixed forms and strong rhythms, their concern for striking images, and their overwhelming interest in subjective emotional states.[8] Most of these compositions are metrically regular. They rely heavily on consonantal rhyme, erudite vocabulary, and Lusitanian grammatical structures. From time to time, the poet experiments with both form and content, introducing hints of irony and an incipient interest in everyday speech rhythms as well as quotidian themes. Nonetheless, the almost obsessive musicality and all-pervasive melancholy of the poems confirm their nineteenth-century heritage.

The death of his mother, father, only sister, and an older brother between 1916 and 1922 sharpened Bandeira's sense of isolation and impending doom. For the rest of his life, he lived alone in a series of rented rooms. And, physically incapable of holding a full-time job, he eked out a living as a translator, newspaper columnist, anthologist, high school teacher, and, somewhat later, professor of Hispano-American literature at the Federal University of Rio de Janeiro. Bandeira paid for the publication of his poetry out of his own pocket until the age of fifty.[9]

The year 1922 saw the revolt of a number of young army lieutenants in Rio de Janeiro, a particularly dramatic reflection of mounting dissatisfaction with the status quo. Both the working class and the ascendant urban bourgeoisie were growing weary of abuses associated with the Old Republic. The coup that eight years later brought Getúlio Vargas to power was the culmination of a growing push on the part of these sectors for economic and political representation. (Vargas would go on to establish himself as virtual dictator in 1937, remaining Brazil's most powerful political figure until his suicide in 1954.)[10]

The *Semana de Arte Moderna,* or Modern Art Week, of 1922 in São Paulo, an exhibition of avant-garde paintings calculated to enrage the academic establishment, was a manifestation in the artistic domain of this more generalized spirit of revolt. The multiarts movement known as *modernismo* which was associated with the exhibition should not be confused with the unrelated movement of the same name in Spanish America.[11] In literature, Brazilian Modernism encompasses diverse currents. Critics have devised numerous classificatory schemes for the various phases of the movement which emerged over the decades following its inception. In extremely simplified terms, Modernism can be understood as a reworking of the sort of experimental elements associated with the European vanguard by Brazilian artists with a strongly nationalistic bent. The first representatives of the movement—theorists Oswald de Andrade and Mário de Andrade and the numerous contributors to the magazines *Klaxon* and *Terra Roxa e Outras Terras*—sought to inject a new and free-spirited cosmopolitanism into an increasingly ossified literary code. At the same time, they wanted to create a specifically Brazilian mode of expressing everyday, socially relevant themes. These twin goals led them to eschew elevated, overtly "lyric" subject matter and language in favor of colloquial speech. Flashes of black humor and an often mordant self-awareness are also characteristic of the movement's initial phase.

Bandeira did not participate directly in Modern Art Week. Although he would later speak of his debts to Modernism, he expressed a number of reservations about the movement during its early years.[12] This ambivalence did not keep others from hailing him as a model. Mário de Andrade's reference to him as Modernism's "Saint John the Baptist" underscores his pioneering role in Brazilian poetry.[13] The appearance of *Libertinism* in 1930 confirmed Bandeira's break with the past. Its rejection of metrical constraints, celebration of everyday subjects, experimentation with clichés and purposefully "incorrect" language, and reliance on humor contrast with the relative stiffness and sentimentality of many of the early compositions.

Six years later, the poet's growing fame found confirmation in the publication of *Homenagem a Manuel Bandeira* (Homage to Manuel Bandeira), a series of critical studies, personal reminiscences, and poems in his honor.[14] The first edition of his collected works appeared in 1940, the year he entered the prestigious Brazilian Academy of Letters. (He would later become the first poet to receive a national decoration.) Thereafter, Bandeira continued to publish poetry. The definitive edition of his collected poems appeared in 1966 under the title *Estrela da Vida Inteira* (Star of a Whole Life).[15] In addition, he translated numerous works from English, French, German, and Spanish,[16] and he continued to contribute essays on matters of contemporary interest (*crônicas*) to newspapers.[17] Critical essays and anthologies of Brazilian poetry as well as editions of the works of Romantic and Parnassian writers also kept appearing.[18]

At the time of his death, Bandeira was one of Brazil's best-known authors. And yet, despite the honors lavished on him, he frequently referred to himself as a minor poet. "The world of great abstractions would always be closed to me," he observed on one occasion. "There was not in me that sort of cauldron in which, through the heat of feeling, moral impulses are transformed into aesthetic impulses.[19] Although he insisted on his "intense desire for participation," only a limited number of his poems focus on social problems or express a spirit of solidarity with a larger community.[20] Age intensified Bandeira's more conservative tendencies, but from the very beginning, those texts that protest the sufferings of the masses could also be interpreted as more general statements of life's absurdity.

The irrepressibly lyric and confessional quality that led Bandeira to refer on at least one occasion to his work as "sentimental singsong" was decidedly not characteristic of the 1960s and 1970s.[21] The rightist military coup of 1964 pushed many intellectuals toward overtly committed forms of artistic expression. The increased censorship and torture prompted by the National Security Act of 1968—often called the "coup within a coup"—gave new impetus to writing with an unmistakably public dimension. At the same time, their desire to break with the subjectivism of the Portuguese lyric tradition led other writers with a less explicit social commitment to search for a new, emphatically "impersonal" voice.[22]

The gradual easing of the most blatant constraints on civil liberties, which culminated in the election of a nonmilitary president in 1984, has fostered reevaluation of twentieth-century literary production. The great majority of present-day writers and critics, including those who favor other styles of poetry, are quick to acknowledge Bandeira's historical importance as well as the aesthetic value of individual poems. They point to the linguistic innovations that mark his writing as well as to his genius for imbuing popular themes with a deeper, more universal meaning. Some of the best recent analyses of the poet have emphasized the unmistakably modern features of his earliest and most apparently conventional compositions.[23]

Undeniably affected by specific events as well as more general intellectual currents of both the nineteenth and twentieth centuries, Bandeira was never fully at home in either period. Were he a lesser poet or a less honest human being, his work might be more consistent. But Bandeira recorded what he felt: an obdurate Romantic in many respects, he was also a grudging modern who viewed his own discomfiture with an ironic eye. More than simple mood swings, the oscillations in his poetry bear witness to conflicting, if ultimately complementary, visions of the world.

THE MOVEMENT OF THE POEMS

The immense bibliography on Bandeira includes numerous specialized studies. Critics have written convincingly on areas as varied as his fascination with the idea of purity, his debts to an older Portuguese lyric tradition, and his particular brand of humor.[24] These often-detailed analyses have illuminated important aspects of the poet's literary production, enhancing appreciation of its range and depth.

Comprehensive overviews of Bandeira's work have been less

numerous. Some of these more general studies provide valuable per-spectives on the corpus, suggesting new directions for further study.[25] Others are primarily descriptive. A number are essentially tributes to the poet. The celebratory character of a good portion of these studies of Bandeira reflects his status as a national monument.[26] Not simply a poet but a Brazilian Everyman to many of his readers, the writer was hailed during his lifetime as a rueful and tender ob-server of homely details. A number of critics have continued to rein-force this characterization to the extent that it tends to overshadow or even obscure other facets of his work.

The relative paucity of general studies owes much to the size and heterogeneity of the corpus. A prolific writer, Bandeira demonstrated an almost overwhelming range of forms and themes. It is not easy to categorize an author who may move from sonnets to concrete poems, from haiku to prose, from ballads to free verse, and then back again, all in the same book. The varied subject matter makes content-oriented identifications equally complicated.

And yet despite the multiplicity that is unquestionably one of Bandeira's hallmarks, the poetry reveals a movement that unites the most seemingly disparate texts. The often radical differences in style and subject are subsumed by a larger, though not always readily apparent, opposition between what might be called transcendence and nontranscendence. "Transcendence" is used here to mean the belief or wish to believe in a reality that goes beyond the individual; "nontranscendence," the acknowledgment, if not acceptance, of bod-ily limits. An awareness of this fundamental tension provides an overarching framework that can accommodate multiple and even conflicting readings of the same poem.

Bandeira's arrangement of individual texts reveals a constant flip-ping back and forth between these two positions.[27] Time and again, a transcendent composition is followed by a nontranscendent poem. The poet himself appears to have envisioned his work as a linear progression, expressing pleasure with critic Otto Maria Carpeaux's description of the corpus as an evolution from "the whole life that could have been and wasn't" to another, ever fuller and more har-monious existence.[28] This discussion nevertheless sees Bandeira's evolution as essentially lateral, arguing that the poet stands apart from the great majority of artists in his enduring ability to find new voices for a single, all-important theme. Although one can divide and subdivide the poems into various phases, the transcendence/non-transcendence opposition runs throughout his work.

The following analysis confirms the presence of this primary ten-sion in a half-dozen apparently quite separate subject categories. It looks briefly at poems concerning Nature, the relationship between men and women, and religious themes and images. It also examines texts that deal with everyday objects and occurrences, the theme of art and the artist, and, finally, the problem of time and mortality.

These subject headings are in no way exhaustive. For instance, one could just as easily consider topics such as Bandeira's treatment of the fantastic, geographic places, folk material, urban life, animals, childhood and children, or family relationships. The goal of this discussion, however, is less thematic analysis than confirmation of an underlying dynamic that the reader can test against the corpus as a whole. Each section begins with a brief exploration of Bandeira's presentation of the particular subject in his earliest writing and then points out the opposing poles between which he alternates in the later work.

Poems about Nature

The natural universe plays a major role in Bandeira's first book, *A Cinza das Horas*. Natural entities—above all, sea and sky—serve as a mirror and an extension of the world of human beings.[29] Because the boundaries between the individual and the cosmic are permeable, Nature offers a potential gateway to infinity.

The poet regularly personifies physical forces in his first three books. The pathetic fallacy is particularly evident in poems such as "A Mata" (The Woods) in which the poet compares a forest, first, to an actress in a tragic pantomime, then to a frenzied mob. The tossing, lurching, writhing trees not only move but react like human beings. They know both a desperate fear and a concealed panic. Eager to learn the earth's deepest secrets, they eavesdrop through their roots' fragile ears.

The extremely close relationship between humans and natural entities is equally evident in other poems that emphasize the individual's place within a larger universe. At first glance, a text like the carefully rhymed "Poemeto Erótico" (Small Erotic Poem) appears to be little more than a comparison of a particular woman's body to a long list of natural entities.[30] But this list is not random. The poet carefully chooses representatives of each of the four elements: earth appears as fruit and flowers, water appears as the clear liquid spiraling into song, and air and fire are both present in the flaming skies of early evening. The result is an assertion of the body's cosmic potential. The loved one not only suggests but incorporates the universe.[31]

This privileged relationship between the social order and Nature erodes, when it does not disappear completely, in later, nontranscendent poems. In the earliest work, any separation between the two is the result of temporary human blindness. In later texts, however, the gulf between them has become unbridgeable. Although, for instance, the fixed refrain as well as the references to soft winds and evening flowers in "Tema e Voltas" (Theme and Variations) suggest older compositions, the vast tranquillity of night is a newly ironic confirmation of human limits. "But why so much suffering" the poet demands at the beginning of each stanza. As pain is now a fact of life, the question has no answer.

While in "Theme and Variations," Nature is simply distant, other nontranscendent poems present natural forces as hostile or perverse. The pared-down vocabulary and immediately obvious rhyme scheme of "A Estrela" (The Star) emphasize the complexity of human desire. When the poet demands to know why a single white star does not descend from the chilly heights to join him, she responds that she glimmers there to nourish his doomed hopes. Similarly, when the Evening Star actually plummets from the heavens into the poet's bed in the brief and ironic "A Estrela e o Anjo" (Star and Angel), his desire remains unsatisfied. Devoid of the "least erotic impulse," the celestial visitor causes two large rosebuds to shrivel and die. Despite the fact that, in both cases, the star is clearly feminine, it would be misleading to equate it with either a particular woman or women as a whole.[32] The choice of a heavenly, instead of human, body as the object of thwarted passion emphasizes the hopeless quality of the hunger for some sort of extramaterial reality.

The poet is more accepting of human limits in other nontranscendent texts. Unrhymed, pointedly antilyrical texts like "Lua Nova" (New Moon) and "Satélite" (Satellite) stand apart from the early compositions in both form and content. The first poem dismisses the full moon—"that sun of vague, noctambular madness"—in favor of another that possesses none of its predecessor's Romantic characteristics. The second text addresses the moon by its scientific designation. "Demetaphorized, demythified, stripped of the old secret of melancholy," the former star of madmen and lovers is now "only, so only satellite."

But if Bandeira rejects his own earlier vision of Nature on some occasions, he continues to insist on its cosmic potential in others. Although, unlike their predecessors, these transcendent compositions permit only fleeting moments of illumination, they provide an effective contrast to the texts we have just seen.

In a number of later poems, a natural entity serves as a paradigm for human behavior. The water in both "Trucidaram o Rio" (They

Murdered the River) and "O Rio" (The River) is an excellent example. The first poem relies on repetition to emphasize the enduring nature of the droplets that will one day be "greater than any river, / vast as the ocean, / strong as ice, / the polar ice / that shatters all before it." The second uses longer lines (decasyllables, in Portuguese) but equally unencumbered language to suggest the water's capacity to mirror both clear and cloudy skies. The poem asserts that the individual should strive to be like the silent river that remains unmoved by circumstance. "If there are stars," he says, "to mirror them. / And if the sky fills with clouds / (after all, they're water too) / to reflect them without sorrow / in its calm depths."

While both rivers reveal traits that Bandeira believes human beings should emulate and are thus clearly metaphoric, we do not find the sort of personification so common in the earliest poems. At the same time, these texts affirm a proximity between the human and the natural universe that is alien to nontranscendent compositions; they posit boundaries between the two that are not found in early compositions.

This more moderate transcendent stance is especially clear in first-person meditations. The mellifluous "Embalo" (Rocking Song) portrays a small boat on open water. Sea and sky merge as the speaker drinks in the salt winds, but the self does not dissolve before this panoramic vision as it does in Bandeira's initial work. The boatman-poet is both one with and separate from the reality that engulfs him. ("I am nothing and yet now / behold me, finite center / of the infinite sphere / of sea and skies that lie beyond.") Although he claims to be "where God is" in the moment, the assertion of his own finiteness suggests the fleeting nature of this privileged state.

Poems about Men and Women

Sexual experience, like Nature, is a potential gateway to infinity in the young Bandeira.[33] By and large, the early poems idealize the loved one. Any disappointment springs from faults within one or both lovers; the poet rarely questions the concept of love itself.

We have already seen how, in "Little Erotic Poem," the body becomes the world. Companion poems like the gravely sonorous "Boda Espiritual" (Spiritual Wedding) offer an even more direct assertion of the transcendent potential of physicality. Whereas the poet possesses the woman metaphorically in the preceding example, here he describes a body that not only inspires but experiences passion. The loved one presses closer, moans, pleads, gasps, and trembles as the speaker caresses the length of her back and observes the quivering of his own hand.

The last line of the poem ("And I love you as one loves a small and lifeless bird") intentionally undercuts the tactile nature of this description. The Portuguese "passarinho morto" possesses a lilting quality absent in the English "small and lifeless bird." (It is entirely absent from the more literal "little dead bird.") This conclusion emphasizes the would-be transformation of physical passion (Bandeira's term is "volúpia") into selfless love ("ternura"). This climactic metamorphosis both justifies the title, "Spiritual Wedding," and relates the poem to others in which physical attraction serves as stepping-stone to another plane of understanding.

The earliest work does offer one or another challenge to this concept. The most notable is the bitingly humorous "Vulgívaga" (Vulgívaga), in which the persona begins and ends by scoffing at the idealization of sex.[34] ("I can't believe that anyone could think of love / as anything but carnal pleasure! / My lover died an alcoholic / and my husband a consumptive.") The irony, adroitly reinforced by the poem's almost rollicking rhythm, contrasts with the customarily solemn, even reverent, view of the relationship between men and women.

Libertinism shatters this mold by presenting sexual attraction as essentially absurd. As in "Vulgívaga," the majority of these poems question or deride the whole notion of romantic love. Now, however, the poet employs one first person rather than appearing to let another figure speak.

Also in contrast to "Vulgívaga," whose mocking stance is unmistakable, many of these poems appear to be lighthearted, innocuous transformations of clichés and colloquial language into an exuberantly free verse.[35] The great majority of critics have treated texts like "Namorados" (Boy and Girl) as stylized parody.[36] In this example, the boy informs his girlfriend that he still has not grown accustomed to her body and face. He then compares her to the striped caterpillars that fascinate small children. When the girl protests the analogy, he dismisses her exclamations with an ostensibly offhand "Antônia, you're so funny! You know, you're crazy."

As so often happens in Bandeira's poetry, however, the dialogue is not so innocent as it first appears. The potentially insulting comparison of the girl to a caterpillar has less to do with her physical appearance than with the essential strangeness of heterosexual relationships. The supposed tenderness of the boy's remarks does not obviate a definite sense of alienation. The caterpillar represents another order of being. (Caterpillars are often considered ugly, but they turn into butterflies or, less glamorous but equally compelling in their transformation, moths.) Just so, the Antônia of the poem remains fundamentally other, making any genuine understanding between the sexes impossible.

The theme of mutual incomprehension reappears in other short, unrhymed poems in *Libertinism*, for example, "Porquinho-da-Índia" (Guinea Pig), "Teresa" (Teresa), and "Mulheres" (Women).[37] "Guinea Pig" stresses the inability of one individual to control another's actions in the figure of the little creature who rebuffs the poet's attentions ("All it wanted was to hide out under the stove.") In "Teresa," the only possible communication between the sexes is a momentary, physical understanding. "Women" suggests that one cannot determine whom one loves.[38] While some readers will find the poet's lament over his inability to love a homely woman offensive, the real point of the poem is the lack of control one has—not only over others but over oneself—in love.

A number of these nontranscendent poems are bitter, even cruel. Others, ultimately no less serious assaults on an old ideal, are decidedly whimsical. The green pool that craves the sunburned body of a certain woman in the insistently rhythmic, repetitious "Piscina" (Pool), for example, has to settle for a plump white moon. Although "A Filha do Rei" (The King's Daughter) looks much like a children's rhyme, the disillusionment it dwells on is an adult's. In the same breath that the poet expresses his longing to observe at length the body of the princess who glides by him, he acknowledges the impossible nature of his desire.

Equally unattainable female figures appear in the "Balada das Três Mulheres do Sabonete Araxá" (Ballad of the Three Women on the Araxá Soap Wrapper), "D. Janaína" (Dona Janaína), and "Estrela da Manhã" (Morning Star).[39] The three soap wrapper muses, the Afro-Brazilian sea goddess resplendent in a bright red swimsuit, and the star that cheerfully sleeps with Greeks as well as Trojans affirm both the power and the limits of the imagination.

Perhaps the single clearest statement of the impossibility of any genuine communication between men and women occurs in the short but pointed "Arte de Amar" (Art of Loving). Here the poet states categorically that the person who wants to experience the joy of love should ignore any nonphysical concern. Because souls can only find satisfaction in God or "in some other world," they, unlike bodies, are "not communicable."

If love is a delusion in nontranscendent compositions, it is the

fundamental truth of human existence in their transcendent counter-
parts, which link body and spirit in a manner reminiscent of the
earliest poems. In the emphatically brief last line of "Pousa a Mão na
Minha Testa" (Rest your Hand on My Forehead), "the only word that
counts" is, once more, "Amor," or Love.

And yet, if this assertion suggests a return to an earlier optimism
about heterosexual relationships, the privileged moment these now
permit is, as in the case of Nature, distinctly transitory. The carefully
matter-of-fact "Art of Loving" contrasts with the immediately preced-
ing "Unidade" (Union), which reaffirms the spiritual dimension of
physicality in a series of extravagant metaphors. Despite linguistic as
well as conceptual links to the earliest compositions, the poem
acknowledges boundaries not operative in these. The titular unity
refers both to the coupling of a man and woman and to a reintegration
of the self through sexual intercourse. The poet begins by describing
a state of alienation. "My soul," he asserts, "was in that instant / out-
side me, far off, very far." The arrival of a particular woman and the
ensuing sexual encounter causes the initially estranged soul to reenter
the body, shaking the speaker "to the core / in the fleeting moment
of union." Although the climactic moment is ephemeral, the soul
does not "spoil things" but indeed makes possible this admittedly
transitory wholeness.

These later celebrations of the body are often more playful than
their forebears. In the unrhymed quatrains of "Nu" (Naked), for
instance, the poet speaks of the light of a woman's knees and navel,
then describes a "perpendicular dive" that brings him face to face
with her naked soul. The later texts are also likely to acknowledge an
essential ambiguity. Thus the sonnet "Peregrinação" (Pilgrimage) pre-
sents a woman who, like one of Picasso's portraits, is actually two
individuals in one. April as well as August, plump as well as slender,
she incarnates conflicting possibilities. "Love perfect and imperfect,"
concludes the poet, "pure and impure . . . / Love of an old adoles-
cent . . . And with so strong / a taste of ash and ripened peaches."

Poems Utilizing Religious Imagery

At no stage in his literary career is Bandeira a religious writer in
the conventional sense. And yet, despite his scant interest in theolo-
gical concerns, he continually seeks some meaning in life. While a
number of the later poems find significance in the everyday world,
most early texts affirm the existence of a reality beyond this world.

In addition, the initial work tends to take for granted a sense of purpose on which some subsequent compositions defiantly insist.

From his first book onward, Bandeira utilizes Christian symbols and figures fairly regularly to express his own feelings and desires. The "Balada de Santa Maria Egipcíaca" (Ballad of Saint Mary of Egypt) is an early example. Bandeira has rewritten the story (and opened the customarily fixed Iberian *romance* form) to reflect his fascination with purity and defilement. In the earliest versions of the story, Mary, a prostitute of Alexandria since the age of twelve, repents while praying before a statue of the Virgin. She then goes into self-imposed exile in the desert. But in Bandeira's recasting of the legend, which is also a twelfth-century ballad, Mary of Egypt is forced to sleep with a boatman in exchange for transportation across the river to the Holy Land. The poem is less about the saint's relationship to God than her triumphant imperviousness to an otherwise degrading experience.[40]

Religious imagery serves a different but still distinctly personal end in later, nontranscendent poems. In fact, some of the harshest judgments in the entire corpus utilize Christian symbols. Far from holding out the promise of spiritual fulfillment, Bandeira derides both human faith in God and God's trust in human beings. The eight-line prose poem "Conto Cruel" (Cruel Story) lives up to its title. When a tranquilizer fails to numb his pain, an elderly man calls out in affectionate trust to a "Sweet Lord Jesus," who does not manifest the slightest concern for his plight. The poet's repetition of the diminutive, which is also a term of endearment ("Jesus Cristinho" instead of "Jesus Cristo" in the last line), provides an ironic foil to the divine disinterest in human hope or suffering.[41]

Not all nontranscendent poems see God as distant or mocking. Sometimes human beings scoff at the divinity. In "Presepe" (Manger Scene), the infant Jesus cries when confronted with "the pain of being human / the horror of being human." The angels' hymns of praise contrast with the profound skepticism of the little donkey who foresees "the futility / of the greatest miracle, / the futility / of every sacrifice." Although here, as in a number of other texts, the regular rhyme and meter partially undermine the explicit message, the poem's mood remains dark.

As in previous sections, the cynicism of many of these nontranscendent texts that employ Christian imagery contrasts with the joyful certainty of other, transcendent compositions. These poems assert the presence of a supernatural force in human affairs. The exultant musicality of "Canto de Natal" (Christmas Carol), a good example of the *sainete* form in Portuguese, provides a striking contrast to the overwhelming pessimism of the manger scene introduced several pages later. Not only does the infant Christ fully accept the human destiny that terrified him in the nontranscendent composition but his triumphant sacrifice promises the redemption of humankind. "For us," says the poem, "he embraces / the sorrows of this life. / All praise and all glory / to the child Christ."[42]

The intersection of the human and the supernatural is still more emphatic on other occasions. In the singsong "Ubiqüidade" (Ubiquity), the omnipresent "You" of the poem is as apparent in the lone sheep that grazes as it is in the human soul. The simplicity of language underscores and intensifies the elemental, all-embracing quality of the life force. "You are in the soul, the senses," the poet affirms, "you are in the spirit, you live / in words and time once over, / you'll live in the sky, you'll live!"

Bandeira's transcendent compositions are not necessarily celebratory. In "Versos para Joaquim" (Poem for Joaquim), the poet asks God why his friend's wife should have been singled out to die. Despite his confidence that Joaquim can be both mother and father to the couple's young children, the loss remains incomprehensible. And yet, at the same time that he declares "the will of the Lord is sometimes hard to accept," he does not deny or even question the existence of an all-knowing deity. The poem portrays God, like Joaquim, as a longtime acquaintance with whom one can choose or choose not to speak.

Poems on Everyday Themes

Although Bandeira initially favors dramatic, often cosmic, themes, everyday details appear in some of his earliest work.[43] Even when his tone and subject are undeniably elevated, the poet may introduce humdrum, even homely, images. "Os Sapos" (The Toads), for example, employs an unlikely amphibian chorus—and an equally improbable fixed metrical pattern—to attack the Parnassian obsession with form.[44] "Debussy," one of Bandeira's first experiments in free verse, imitates the to-and-fro motion of a ball of yarn dangling from the hand of a sleepy child.[45] "Menino Carvoeiros" (Little Coalmen) depicts a street scene. Various other early poems, almost always experimental in form as well as content, utilize familiar settings, for instance, the country road in "Noite Morta" (Dead of Night).

And yet, while these texts faithfully record ordinary people in readily recognizable surroundings, these elements—except perhaps in "Debussy"—retain heavily symbolic properties. "Dead of Night" begins as a matter-of-fact description of a road where toads gulp down mosquitoes. The concluding line, however, makes clear that the poet is speaking "not of this night, but of another, larger."

Beginning with *Libertinism,* a substantial percentage of Bandeira's poems deal with day-to-day realities less as symbols than as objects of concern in their own right.[46] The nontranscendent compositions alternate between an insistence that the here-and-now is all one could ever need and the rueful or bitter affirmation that this world is all one can ever know.

The first of two poems based on a popular song entitled "Belo Belo" (Lovely Lovely) adopts the first position, resolutely affirming the self-sufficiency of the material world. Although references to "the fire of constellations extinct now for millennia" and the "purest tears" of dawn recall an older poetic legacy, Bandeira claims to reject both ecstasy and torment, observing wryly that the gifts of angels are useless ("Angels don't understand human beings"). Proclaiming himself content with life as he finds it, he concludes by asking nothing more than "the pleasure of being able to experience the simplest things."

Other, often overtly antilyrical, celebrations of the present poke fun at the desire for something beyond what meets the eye. Although "Comentário Musical" (Musical Commentary) begins with a litany of breezes from far-off ports, the "musical gloss upon the landscape" turns out to be nothing more—or less—than the shrill whistle of a neighbor's pet. ("My downstairs neighbor has just bought a pet monkey," the poet explains.) The tiny, strident creature, a caricature of humankind, effectively undercuts the longing for a boundless seascape, which the introduction seems to promise.

The hint of ambiguity present in this poem deepens in other nontranscendent compositions. While Bandeira continues to celebrate the "canticle of certainties" that the blacksmith beats out every morning in "O Martelo" (The Hammer), he portrays a far less attractive reality in other poems. In "Pensão Familiar" (Two-Star Hotel), the sun scorches the flowers in the courtyard of the very ordinary boardinghouse in which the little cat is "the only superior creature."[47] The infectious laughter of the small Indian girl in "Cunhantã" (the indigenous word for "young girl") only underscores the cruelty of the stepmother who rubs the child's forehead in the live embers of a fire. The delicious black humor of the prose poem "Tragédia Brasileira" (Brazilian Tragedy) cannot obviate the fact that a murder occurs.

There is nothing funny about poems like the painfully spare "O

Bicho" (The Creature).[48] The living thing that pawed through the refuse in the poet's courtyard was not dog, cat, or rat but "my God, was a man." The interjection "my God" ("meu Deus," in Portuguese) reflects both the speaker's horror and the irony of the situation. Supposedly molded in the image of a divine creator, the human being in this poem has been reduced by hunger to the level of a beast.

The brutality of several of these everyday scenes leads the poet to conclude that life is devoid of any meaning. The use of repetition in "Momento num Café" (Moment in a Café)—"caught up in life, / absorbed in life, / confident of life"—emphasizes the mechanical reaction to the death of the customers in a neighborhood tavern. Only one of the men really sees the passing cortege. In dismissing human experience as "a fierce and senseless agitation" and a "betrayal," he is clearly speaking for Bandeira, at least in this case. The similarly negative "Entrevista" (Interview) begins with a verbal explosion: "Life that dies and that subsists / fickle, ludicrous, grasping, vile / defiled!" Should a reporter chance to ask what he finds loveliest in "this thankless world," the poet would be hard-pressed to answer. But the saddest aspect is unquestionably "a woman— / any woman with child." Although once again rhyme and meter provide a counterpoint to content, the poem is startling in its overwhelming bitterness.

Scornful assertions of absurdity find a balance in transcendent compositions that insist on the enigmatic nature of seemingly ordinary objects and activities. In stripping away an often deceptive exterior, these poems affirm life's meaning. The contrast between appearance and reality is particularly clear in texts such as the quietly rhythmic "Maçã" (Apple). The single fruit that sits between a knife and fork in a decidedly modest hotel room resembles "a withered breast" from one angle, thus suggesting the death and destruction on which so many nontranscendent poems insist. From another view, however, the apple evokes a navel from which the umbilical cord still hangs. "Crimson like divine love," the fruit contains innumerable small seeds that belie the appearance of decay.

The elusive, ultimately positive nature of the physical world is still more evident in the irregularly rhymed quatrains of "Água-Forte" (Aqua Fortis), in which an etching of a woman's body leads the poet to meditate on the mystery of her sex.[49] ("All well concealed / beneath the guise / of a simple print," he asserts.) The concluding lines, "head-on, from the side, / black on white" (a couplet in Portuguese), reinforce the promise of concealed meaning. Like the single rose on a branch in "Eu Vi Uma Rosa" (I Saw a Rose), the representation of the woman is compelling in its apparent simplicity.

While fruit, flowers, and the female body are used to affirm life's meaning in the earliest poems, the later work utilizes a number of less conventional objects and images toward this same end. The peddlers of assorted trinkets in the free verse "Camelôs" (Street Vendors) do more than add life and color to the city streets. Along with wooden monkeys on a stick and fountain pens that "will never write a blessed word," these "demigods of trifles" offer weary passersby a lesson in the "heroic myths of childhood." Similarly, the sordid aspects of the alley in "Última Canção do Beco" (Parting Song of the Alley) only intensify its beauty. "Alley born in the shadow / of convent walls," the poet says in the last of seven stanzas that are Portuguese *redondilhas*, "you are like life that is sacred / despite its disappointments. / That's why I sing to you to say / so long / so long forever!"[50]

Poems about Art and the Artist

Bandeira sometimes uses familiar scenes and ordinary objects to express his views on art and the artist. As could be expected, the early work reveals an essentially Romantic perspective. Although he employs a variety of everyday elements, he continues to see art as the property of a spiritual elite.

Much like the small toad who weeps hidden from the world in "Os Sapos" or the lone clump of bamboo that remains off to one side in "A Mata" (The Woods), the consumptive typographer in "Na Rua do Sabão" (Soap Street) stands apart from his peers. Lovely in its fragility, the paper balloon he constructs defies the jeers of the street urchins as well as official prohibitions. Buoyed by its creator's breath, it floats not only higher but farther from the city, finally falling into the clear and implicitly boundless waters of the high seas.

The peddler who offers his brightly colored wares in "Balõezinhos" (Balloons) provides a contrast to the neighboring fish stands and grain stalls where people haggle over pennies. The children who surround him are likewise distinguished from the adults in their recognition that the peddler's apparently useless wares "are the only thing / that counts, that really matters." The "fixed circle of desire and wonder" that they form about the man further isolates him from the flurry of commercial activities. Thus, while the art form here is distinctly nonelitist—a simple balloon—the poet continues to insist on the privileged character of art.

This vision of art as the property of a spiritual elite continues in "Bonheur Lyrique," where the poet compares himself to the poor child who creates a solitary fantasy. In "Poética" (Poetics), however, whose free verse form contrasts with the chiming rhyme of "Bonheur Lyrique," he declares himself sick of a cautious, "civil service" lyricism. Denouncing academic conventions ("Down with purists!" he exclaims), he calls for a poetry that will describe the world-as-is.[51] "I prefer the lyricism of madmen," he says, "the lyricism of drunks / the difficult and bitter / lyricism of the drunk, / the lyricism of Shakspeare's clowns."

Shakespeare's clowns are not ordinary clowns, let alone ordinary people. Nonetheless, to the extent that the poet categorically refuses to have anything more to do with "lyricism that isn't liberation," "Poetics" represents an important shift in perspective. No longer a product of the nineteenth-century Ivory Tower, art now resides in the faithful recording of experiences that may be difficult and painful.

The emphatically antilyrical "Nova Poética" (New Poetics) takes this concept a step farther. While in the preceding example the poet suggests that life is not always pleasant or easy, here he compares it to the mud that soils a man's carefully starched white suit. The purpose of art is to bear witness to these assaults on the unsuspecting. "A poem should be like mud on cloth," the speaker declares. "It should drive the complacent reader wild." Although acknowledging that poetry "is also dew," he reserves this definition for the exceptionally lucky or relentlessly naive. For all except "good little girls, the brightest stars, virgins a hundred percent virgin, and former sweethearts who manage to grow old without a hint of malice," life—and art—are "sordid." The artist is no longer a creator of beauty but he in whose work the "smudge" or "dirty mark" of life appears.

The sardonic tone of this last example is wholly foreign to other transcendent poems that portray the artist as witness to, or actual participant in, the mysteries of life. "Sacha e o Poeta" (Sacha and the Poet) chronicles an excursion to a thoroughly marvelous realm in an exuberant, partially nonsense language.[52] The poet in the text descends to the earth's burning core, rises to the highest cloud, and transforms himself into the Afro-Brazilian prankster deity, Exu. His audience and accomplice is the infant girl, Sacha, who transmits to him through the Morse code of baby talk "the latest message of the angels." (Not surprising from what we have seen of Bandeira, in the very next poem, "Jacqueline," the woman's name denies the existence of these celestial entities.)[53]

Although "Sacha and the Poet" assigns poetry the sort of power it possesses in earlier compositions, the humor and hyperbole of the text are alien to its predecessors. Furthermore, there is no mention of an uncomprehending crowd; the artist's privileged vision no longer isolates him from other human beings. Although art continues to imply a special vision, its worth lies increasingly in its effect on others in the larger world from which it springs.

"Mozart no Céu" (Mozart in Heaven) employs insouciant colloquial language ("What gives? What doesn't?") to describe the musician's entrance into paradise. The initial run-on sentence compares him to a circus performer "making extravagant / pirouettes on the back of a dazzling white horse."[54] As never-before-heard melodies begin to soar on lines above the staff, the ineffable contemplation ceases for a split second. The Virgin Mary then kisses Mozart on the forehead, making him "the youngest angel." On one level, the poem is sheer play; on another, an affirmation of art's power. The musician does not owe his entrance into heaven to any moral quality but rather to the ability of his music to move a particular, in this case, celestial, audience.

The artist is thus no longer the solitary, often sorrowful figure of early poems. Even though poetry remains all but synonymous with suffering in texts such as "Infância" (Childhood), the knowledge of darkness produces its own form of clarity. "As Três Marias" (The Three Marys) begins with a description of a dark landscape full of monsters such as headless mules and witches who whisper lurid secrets to the wind. The speaker, however, is able to step back from this scene whose disturbing phantasmagoric quality is undercut by the poem's lilting rhythm. "But what of it?" he demands. "There are yet darker regions / I've known. I am a poet and I carry / in my soul, I carry / the three stars, I carry / the three Marys!" The presence of this light within (the Three Marys is a constellation in the Southern Hemisphere) suggests art's power over the most compelling forms of death and corruption.

Poems about Time and Mortality

On some level, all of Bandeira's poems are about time and mortality. Nevertheless, from the very beginning, some compositions deal with these subjects far more directly than others.

The tightly rhymed "Epígrafe" (Epigraph), which prefaces Bandeira's first book of poetry, expresses a concern with loss that will reappear in varied form throughout his work. The poet speaks of an early happiness shattered by the evil genius of life that leaves him nothing more than the "handful of cold ashes" that provides the title for the book.[55]

Despite the melancholy, if not morbid, tone that characterizes much of the early poetry, the majority of these texts do not question the concept of immortality. They are thus unlike later, nontranscendent compositions in which time not only occasions loss but a series of transformations that climax in death.

In "Passeio em São Paulo" (A Walk through São Paulo), a kind of verbal montage that combines lines from poems by Mário de Andrade with an observation of the present-day city, "everything is new."[56] Even those vestiges of the past that have survived are not the same. The once-pink angel, for instance, now has a patina of soot. The changes in the metaliterary "Antônia" are similar but even more profound. Not only is Antônia dead, her house long since demolished, but the poet himself is "no longer the one who loved Antônia and Antônia didn't love."

The initial poems treat the loss of a loved one or the sudden perception of personal mortality as an impetus for an extended meditation on this life. But with *Libertinism*, the poet shifts his focus to the finality of death. An army bugler's rendition of "Taps" over the war hero's grave in "O Major" (The Major) represents an emphatic rejection of the nonessential. But it is also an assault on the concept of an afterlife. Unlike its predecessors, the poem offers no suggestion of anything beyond the moment—no glimmering horizon, no lapping of some far-off sea. It thus foreshadows later texts such as the hypnotically repetitious "Boi Morto" (Dead Ox), in which the bloated carcass drifts downstream devoid of "feeling, form or any meaning."

Some of the later poems suggest that the self lives on in other people. In the meditative "A Mário de Andrade Ausente" (To Mário de Andrade, Absent), the poet assures his recently departed friend, "Your life goes on / within this life you lived." This definition of eternity, however, provides little comfort in other poems. "We all die twice," the poet declares at the outset of "Names," pointedly adopting the plural. Time not only erodes the flesh but it slowly robs the name of its associative power "until one day we realize / with a shock of surprise (perhaps remorse?) / that the beloved name now sounds like all the rest." Although the letters chiseled into stone resist oblivion longer than the body, they too are doomed to the extinction from which there is no escape.

The promise of eternity pervading Bandeira's earliest work thus pales or disappears in these nontranscendent texts. Yet while many of these poems summarily dismiss "the snuffed-out soul" (the line is from "Moment in a Café"), a smaller number convey a luminous acceptance of mortality. "Preparação para a Morte" (Preparation for Death) uses a succession of half-echoes to affirm the miraculous and infinite nature of space and time. Although human memory and consciousness are equally worthy of wonder, they do not share this quality of infinitude. No miracle itself, Death is nonetheless "blessed" because it makes life fragile and therefore precious.

Again, these varying confirmations of mortality are balanced by other, transcendent poems that affirm the power of memory over time and the survival of the individual after death. The separation of past and present so evident in the preceding illustrations is less clear-cut in these compositions. Despite the fact that time brings change, some things endure. The bipartite structure of "Christmas Poem" emphasizes the tension between appearance and reality that we have already observed in poems about heterosexual love. The white-haired man reflected in the mirror harbors within him a child who "would still like to leave his slippers behind the door" for the Christmas Fairy to fill. Likewise, in "Última Canção do Beco" (Parting Song of the Alley), the building about to be demolished will continue to exist "not like an imperfect form / in this world of appearances" but as a part of eternity with the poet's personal possessions "intact, suspended in the air!"

Loss paradoxically ensures not only survival but increase in other transcendent compositions. In the intensely melodic "Canção do Vento e da Minha Vida" (Song of the Wind and of My Life), the wind sweeps away natural objects such as fruits, leaves, and flowers; then lights, music, and perfume. In the process, the poet's life becomes progressively fuller. The wind next makes off with more abstract qualities—dreams, friendship, love—with the same inexplicable multiplication effect. Finally, it lays siege to all before it, occasioning an all-encompassing plenitude.

Transcendent poems affirm the soul's enduring nature. Explicit denials of an afterlife find their counterpart in equally explicit affirmations. After a wounded sparrow dies in the almost aphoristic "Pardalzinho" (Sparrow), the bird's young friend buries the body in her garden. The soul, however, flies off to sparrow heaven.

The boundaries between the visible and the invisible are not hard and fast in many transcendent compositions. The shift from the affirmative to the interrogatory mode in the conclusion of the deceptively slight "Cabedelo" introduces a hint of doubt about the finality of death. "Sister, little sister, you weren't there with me," says the poet. "Were you?"[57]

The belief, or wish to believe, in a hereafter is often expressed in seemingly lighthearted fashion. In the tender, almost whimsical "Ovalle," the poet now suggests that his friend has grown a long white beard in order to enter Eternity with suitable decorum. The likewise apparently playful "Programa para depois de Minha Morte" (Program for after My Death) proposes a full schedule of activities for the afterlife. In dramatic contrast to "Preparation for Death," which immediately precedes it, the poem sees earthly existence not as a flash of consciousness ending in oblivion but as a necessary preface to eternity.[58]

Transcendence and Nontranscendence in Bandeira's Poetry

The transcendence/nontranscendence opposition that we have examined dominates Bandeira's work. This obsessive concern would quickly become self-imitation in a lesser poet. And yet, although Bandeira does repeat himself on more than one occasion, his command of myriad voices imbues a potentially static opposition with a dynamic force. In line with his belief that the only type of sincerity that art demands is "that of the moment," he devises multiple and sometimes contradictory answers to an all-consuming question.[59]

In the extended string of lyric recollections of his childhood home entitled "Evocação do Recife" (Evocation of Recife), the poet employs the verb "politonar" to describe the voices of a group of girls. The same term, which refers to the use of two or more tonalities simultaneously in a musical composition, might well apply to the corpus as a whole. Reading Bandeira is a little like watching a child pluck the petals from a daisy, murmuring "Loves me, loves me not." But while the petals fall away until the child gets an answer, one poem echoes in the next.

The poet speaks of his fondness for counterpoint. "To take a theme and elaborate upon it, or as in the sonata form, to take two themes and oppose them, make them battle, collide, wound, and tear each other apart before awarding the victory to one or, on the contrary, to set them at peace in a wholly harmonious understanding. . . . I believe there can be no greater pleasure in the realm of art."[60] The tension in his poetry, however, is far more than a literary exercise.

This earth, that sky; that sky, this earth; Bandeira plays off one against the other, half-surprised when at times they merge in a pulse of light.

NOTES

1. There is a massive bibliography on Bandeira and his poetry in Portuguese. The single most complete, up-to-date listing of sources is *Manuel Bandeira: O Amigo do Rei* (Rio de Janeiro: Biblioteca Nacional, 1986), which includes works both by and about the poet. For articles in periodicals, the one area in which the guide is weak, see *Manuel Bandeira*, ed. Sônia Brayner, Coleção Fortuna Crítica 5 (Rio de Janeiro: Civilização Brasileira/Instituto Nacional do Livro, Ministério de Educação e Cultura, 1980), 27–29.

Book-length studies of the poet include Stefan Baciu, *Manuel Bandeira de Corpo Inteiro*, Coleção Documentos Brasileiros 122 (Rio de Janeiro: José Olympio, 1966); Joaquim-Francisco Coelho, *Biopoética de Manuel Bandeira* (Recife: Editora Massangana/Fundação Joaquim Nabuco, 1981), and *Manuel Bandeira, Pre-Modernista* (Rio de Janeiro: José Olympio; Brasília: Instituto Nacional do Livro, Ministério de Educação e Cultura, 1982); Ruy Ribeiro Couto, *Dois Retratos de Manuel Bandeira* (Rio de Janeiro: Livraria São José, 1960); Júlio Castañón Guimarães, *Manuel Bandeira: Beco e Alumbramento* (São Paulo: Brasiliense, 1984); Eugênio Gomes, *Manuel Bandeira Poeta Xexéu* (Salvador: A Nova Graphica, 1927); *Homenagem a Manuel Bandeira: Poemas, Estudos Críticos, Depoimentos e Impressões* (Rio de Janeiro: Jornal do Commercio, 1936); Aderbal Jurema, Domingos Carvalho da Silva, and Anderson Braga Horta, *Semana de Estudos sobre Manuel Bandeira* (Brasília: Centro de Ensino Unificado de Brasília, 1982); Adolfo Casais Monteiro, *Manuel Bandeira* (Rio de Janeiro: Ministério de Educação e Cultura, 1952); Emanuel de Morais, *Manuel Bandeira* (*Análise e Interpretação Literária*), Coleção Documentos Brasileiros 115 (Rio de Janeiro: José Olympio, 1962); and Giovanni Pontiero, *Manuel Bandeira: Visão Geral de Sua Obra*, trans. Terezinha Prado Galante (Rio de Janeiro: José Olympio, 1986).

2. Fleeing Napoleon, the Portuguese king, João VI, came to Brazil with the entire court in 1808. When he returned to Portugal in 1821, he left his heir, Dom Pedro, who declared himself emperor of an independent Brazil a year later. A military coup in 1889 replaced the empire with a republic.

For an English-language overview of key developments in Brazilian history, see E. Bradford Burns, *A History of Brazil* (New York: Columbia University Press, 1970), which includes a useful bibliography, 423–431.

3. Manuel Bandeira, "Itinerário de Pasárgada," *Poesia Completa e Prosa*, 2d ed. (Rio de Janeiro: José Aguilar Editora, 1967), 42. Originally published by *Jornal de Letras* in 1954, this account, on which I have relied heavily, sheds considerable light on the poet's personal and artistic evolution. All translations are my own.

4. Besides the numerous articles on music and the graphic arts which he contributed to newspapers and magazines, Bandeira was the author of *Mário de Andrade, Animador da Cultura Musical Brasileira* (Rio de Janeiro: Teatro Municipal, 1954), which discusses Mário de Andrade's role in modern Brazilian musical history.

Bandeira's predisposition toward music is obvious in his poetry. Not only are a large number of poems entitled "song" ("canção" or "cantiga") but dozens of his texts have been set to music. For a listing of these, see *Manuel Bandeira: O Amigo do Rei*, 33–35.

5. For a study of the effects of tuberculosis on Bandeira's poetry see Túlio Hostílio Montenegro, "A Tuberculose na Poesia de Manuel Bandeira," *Minas Gerais (Suplemento Literário)*, 19 October 1968. It is interesting to consider the poems in the light of Susan Sontag's *Illness as Metaphor* (New York: Vintage Books, 1978).

6. Éluard speaks of Bandeira's early influence on him in "Foi Manuel Bandeira quem me iniciou na Poesia: Paul Éluard rompe um Silêncio de Dois Anos," *Jornal de Letras*, 3, 20 (1951):1.

Bandeira wrote a series of poems entitled "Poemetos Eróticos" ("Little Erotic Poems") while at Clavadel, but he lost the manuscript on leaving and was unable to reproduce it from memory.

7. For a description and examples of Brazilian Parnassian and Symbolist poets, see Bandeira's own *Antologia dos Poetas Brasileiros da Fase Parnasiana* (Rio de Janeiro: Ministério da Educação e Saúde, 1938) and his *Antologia dos Poetas Brasileiros da Fase Simbolista* (Rio de Janeiro: Tecnoprint, 1965). A short but useful description of these movements with corresponding bibliography appears in *Presença da Literatura Brasileira*, II, ed. Antônio Cândido and J. Aderaldo Castello, 4th rev. ed. (São Paulo: Difel, 1972), 107–133.

8. These features are charted and analyzed on a quantitative as well as qualitative basis in Norma Goldstein, "O Crepuscular Maior: Manuel Bandeira," 96–171, in her *Do Penumbrismo ao Modernismo (O Primeiro Bandeira e Outros Poetas Significativos)*, Ensaios 95 (São Paulo: Ática, 1983).

9. Bandeira's first five books of poetry had an average edition of 200 copies. *Libertinagem*, one of the landmarks in Brazilian literary history, had 500. Only 47 of the projected 50 copies of *Estrela da Manhã* (Morning Star) were published because "the Press ran out of paper."

10. A good overview of this period is available in Jordan M. Young, *The Brazilian Revolution of 1930 and the Aftermath* (New Brunswick: Rutgers University Press, 1967).

11. There is an exhaustive bibliography on Brazilian Modernism. For an English-language account, see Wilson Martins, *The Modernist Idea; A Critical Survey of Brazilian Writing in the Twentieth Century* (New York: New York University Press, 1970), and John Nist, *The Modernist Movement in Brazil* (Austin: University of Texas Press, 1967). A number of Portuguese texts with introductions and explanatory material in English appear in *An Anthology of Brazilian Modernist Poetry*, ed. Giovanni Pontiero (Oxford: Pergamon Press, 1969).

A few of the many critical works in Portuguese that merit attention are Mário da Silva Brito, *História do Modernismo Brasileiro* (São Paulo: Saraiva, 1958), and Luiz Carlos Lessa, *O Modernismo Brasileiro e a Língua Portuguesa*, 2d rev. ed. (Rio de Janeiro: Grifo, 1976). For the larger cultural and historical context of Modernism, see the short but useful work by José Guilherme Merquior, "A Estética do Modernismo do Ponto de Vista da História da Cultura," 77–102, in his *Formalismo e Tradição Moderna: O Problema da Arte na Crise da Cultura* (Rio de Janeiro: Forense-Universitária, 1974). Bandeira's position within the movement is particularly clear in *Poetas do Modernismo: Antologia Crítica*, 6 vols., ed. Leodegário Amarante de Azevedo, 2 vols. (Brasília: Ministério de Educação e Cultura, 1972). The section on Bandeira, with a preface by Bella Jozef, appears in Vol. II, 45–131. For additional references to the Modernist movement, consult *Modernismo Brasileiro: Bibliografia, 1918–1971* (Rio de Janeiro: Divisão de Publicações e Divulgação, 1972).

12. Bandeira speaks of his connections to Modernism in *Itinerário*, 97–100.

13. Bandeira and Mário de Andrade had a long and close relationship. After the latter's death, Bandeira published the former's letters to him in *Cartas a Manuel Bandeira (Pref. e Notas de Manuel Bandeira)* (Rio de Janeiro: Edições de Ouro, 1966).

14. *Homenagem a Manuel Bandeira: Poemas, Estudos Críticos, Depoimentos e Impressões* (Rio de Janeiro: Jornal do Commercio, 1936).

15. Bandeira, *Estrela*. The volume brings together *A Cinza das Horas* (Rio de Janeiro: Jornal do Commercio, 1917); *Carnaval* (Rio de Janeiro: Jornal do Commercio, 1919); *O Ritmo Dissoluto* (Rio de Janeiro: Revista de Língua Portuguesa, 1924); *Libertinagem* (Rio de Janeiro: Pongetti, 1930); *Estrela da Manhã* (Ministério de Educação e Saúde, 1936); *Lira dos Cinqüent'Anos* (Rio de Janeiro: Companhia Carioca de Artes Gráficas, 1940); *Belo Belo* (Rio de Janeiro: Casa do Estudante do Brasil, 1948); *Opus 10* (Niterói: Hipocampo, 1952); *Estrela da Tarde* (Salvador: Editora Dinamene, 1960); plus *Mafuá do Malungo* (Barcelona: personal edition of João Cabral de Melo Neto, 1948) and *Poemas Traduzidos*; plus sections entitled "Duas Canções do Tempo do Beco," "Louvações," "Composições," "Ponteios," and "Preparação para a Morte."

16. Bandeira's translations include Shakespeare's *Macbeth*, Schiller's *Maria Stuart*, and Bertolt Brecht's *The Caucasian Chalk Circle*. A number of his verse translations (authors such as Goethe, Antonio Machado, Rainer Maria Rilke, e.e. cummings, Baudelaire, Emily Dickinson, and García Lorca) were published in *Poemas Traduzidos* (Rio de Janeiro: Revista Acadêmica, 1945) and *Poemas Traduzidos (Ronsard, Rainer Maria Rilke, Goethe e Outros)* (Porto Alegre: Globo, 1948). They reappear in *Estrela da Vida Inteira, Poesias Reunidas* (Rio de Janeiro: José Olympio, 1966). For an English-language assessment of Bandeira's translations from the German, see Juan C. Sager, "A Brazilian Poet's Approach to the Translation of German Poets," *Babel: International Journal of Translation* 12 (1966):198–204.

17. A number of Bandeira's prose pieces are reproduced in *Andorinha, Andorinha* (Rio de Janeiro: José Olympio, 1965). A selection appears in *Manuel Bandeira: Prosa*, ed. Antonio Carlos Villaça (São Paulo: Agir, 1983). Collections

of his contributions to various newspapers as well as weekly radio programs sponsored by the Brazilian Ministry of Education appear in *Flauta de Papel* (Rio de Janeiro: Alvorada Edições de Arte, 1957), *Quadrante* (Rio de Janeiro: Editora do Autor, 1963), *Os Reis Vagabundos e mais 50 Crônicas* (Rio de Janeiro: Editora do Autor, 1966), and *Colóquio Unilateralmente Sentimental* (Rio de Janeiro: Distribuidora Record, 1968). For a fuller listing of Bandeira's prose, see *Manuel Bandeira: O Amigo do Rei,* 16–25.

18. Bandeira's editions are, in chronological order, *Antologia dos Poetas Brasileiros da Fase Romântica* (Rio de Janeiro: Ministério da Educação e Saúde, 1937), *Antologia dos Poetas Brasileiros da Fase Parnasiana, Poesias* (de Alphonsus de Guimaraens) (Rio de Janeiro: Ministério de Educação e Saúde, 1938), *Sonetos Completos e Poemas Escolhidos* (de Antero de Quental) (Rio de Janeiro: Editora Livros de Portugal, 1942), *Obras-Primas da Lírica Brasileira* (São Paulo: Martins, 1943), *Obras Poéticas de Gonçalves Dias* (São Paulo: Editora Nacional, 1944), *Antologia dos Poetas Brasileiros Bissextos Contemporâneos* (Rio de Janeiro: Editora Zélio Valverde, 1946), *Rimas* (de José Albano) (Rio de Janeiro: Pongetti, 1948), *Gonçalves Dias* (Rio de Janeiro: Agir, 1958), *Poesia do Brasil* (Rio de Janeiro: Editora do Autor, 1963), *O Rio de Janeiro em Prosa e Verso* (co-author Carlos Drummond de Andrade) (Rio de Janeiro: José Olympio, 1965), and *Antologia dos Poetas Brasileiros da Fase Simbolista* (Rio de Janeiro: Teenoprint, 1965).

For a discussion of Bandeira as literary critic, see Giovanni Pontiero, "Manuel Bandeira in the Role of Literary Critic," *Annali* 20, no. 1 (1978):203–240.

One of Bandeira's studies, *Apresentação da Poesia Brasileira,* is available in English as *Brief History of Brazilian Literature,* trans. Ralph Edward Dimmick (Washington, D.C.: Pan-American Union, 1958).

19. Bandeira, *Itinerário,* 49. See also his "Depoimento de um Inocente de Flamengo" in *Os Reis Vagabundos,* 81–83, in which he bemoans his lack of "elevação moral" (moral elevation) and expresses admiration for the socially committed poems of Éluard, Aragon, Neruda, and Carlos Drummond de Andrade.

20. *Itinerário,* 106. Bandeira includes among his poems with a social message "Trucidaram o Rio" (They Murdered the River), "O Martelo" (The Hammer), and "No Vosso e em Meu Coração" (In Your Heart and Mine).

21. Bandeira speaks of "a versalhada sentimentalona que fiz, em suma, porque não pude fazer outra coisa" (the sentimental singsong that I wrote, in sum, because I couldn't write anything else) in his *Crônicas da Província do Brasil* (Rio de Janeiro: Civilização Brasileira, 1937), 116.

For a particularly clear expression of this self-deprecating attitude in poetic form, see "Auto-Retrato" in *Estrela da Vida Inteira,* 331.

22. See Lêdo Ivo, "Lembranças de Manuel Bandeira," in his *Teoria e Celebração* (São Paulo: Duas Cidades, 1976), 88, for a suggestion of changing attitudes toward Bandeira.

A number of new currents in Brazilian poetry are exemplified in the English-language anthology of recent Brazilian poetry, *Brazilian Poetry (1950–*

1980), ed. Emanuel Brasil and William Jay Smith (Middletown, Conn.: Wesleyan University Press, 1983).

The work of contemporary Brazilian poets is published on a regular basis by the Editora do Escritor (São Paulo) and Nova Fronteira (Rio de Janeiro).

23. For particularly good studies of the early work, see Goldstein, *Do Penumbrismo*, and Coelho, *Manuel Bandeira, Pre-Modernista*. See also Benedito Nunes, "Resenha de *Manuel Bandeira Pre-Modernista* por Joaquim-Francisco Coelho," *Colóquio: Letras* 74 (1983):111–112, for an explanation of the need for further studies of Bandeira's first three books.

24. Bandeira's debt to the Portuguese classics is the subject of Franklin de Oliveira, "O Medievalismo de Bandeira: A Eterna Elegia," in *Manuel Bandeira*, ed. Sônia Brayner, 235–262; Maria da Conceição Vilhena, "As Duas 'Cantigas Medievais' de Manuel Bandeira," *Revista do Instituto de Estudos Brasileiros* 17 (1975):51–66; and Jayro José Xavier, *Camões e Manuel Bandeira* (Brasília: Ministério de Educação e Cultura, Departamento de Assuntos Culturais, Programa Especial UFF-FCRB, 1973). Sônia Brayner analyzes Bandeira's use of humor in one poem in "O *Humour* Bandeiriano ou as Histórias de um Sabonete" in *Manuel Bandeira*, 340–345.

25. Truly excellent overviews of Bandeira are available in the introduction to *Estrela da Vida Inteira* by Antônio and Gilda Cândido (de Mello e Souza), l–lxx, in Affonso Romano de Sant'Anna, "Manuel Bandeira: Do Amor Místico e Perverso pela Santa e a Prostituta à Família Mítica Permissiva e Incestuosa," 201–256, in his *O Canibalismo Amoroso: O Desejo e a Interdição em Nossa Cultura Através da Poesia* (São Paulo: Brasiliense, 1984), and in Adrien Roig, "Manuel Bandeira, ou o Menino Pai do Poeta," 39–68, in his *Modernismo e Realismo: Mário de Andrade, Manuel Bandeira, Raul Pompeia* (Rio de Janeiro: Presença, 1981).

26. Gary Brower sums up this attitude very well in his reference to Bandeira as "a national treasure like the 'bossa nova' or the Corcovado" ("Graphics, Phonics, and the 'Concrete Universal' in Manuel Bandeira's Concretist Poetry," 19).

27. Antônio and Gilda Cândido underscore this back-and-forth motion in their introduction to *Estrela*. The tension they perceive, however, is not between transcendence and nontranscendence but between "that which adheres strictly to the real world" and "that which attempts to subvert it through a voluntary deformation" [my translation]. For them, then, the fantastic is one of two positions; for me, it is essentially raw material that lends itself to multiple, sometimes conflicting uses. I also find Bandeira's adherence to "the real world" more ambiguous than their summary might suggest.

28. The poet comments on Carpeaux's assessment in *Itinerário*, 132. "The whole life that could have been and wasn't" (a vida inteira que poderia ter sido e que não foi) is a reference to the last line of Bandeira's poem, "Pneumotórax" (Pneumothorax).

29. For a useful discussion of the water imagery that can be found throughout the corpus, see Octávio Mello Alvarenga, "'Água' na Poesia de

Manuel Bandeira," 177–183, in his *Mitos e Valores* (Rio de Janeiro: Instituto Nacional do Livro, 1956).

30. Only one of the objects in the poem, the wedding veil, is not drawn from Nature. Bandeira may have associated the veil with the orange blossoms that immediately precede it since Brazilian brides traditionally carry these flowers.

31. See Múcio Leão, "A Natureza e a Mulher nos Versos de Manuel Bandeira," in *Homenagem a Manuel Bandeira,* 121–126. For a broader background against which to measure the early Bandeira's attitudes toward Nature and the human relationship to natural forces, the reader may find useful Jerome J. McGann, *The Romantic Ideology: A Critical Investigation* (Chicago: University of Chicago Press, 1983).

32. For a fuller discussion of this point, see Candace Slater, "Stars and Other Heavenly Bodies in the Poetry of Manuel Bandeira," in *Commemorative Series* 9.

33. Useful background to the consideration of Bandeira's attitude toward sexual love and women is *The Female Body in Western Culture: Contemporary Perspectives,* ed. Susan Rubin Suleiman (Cambridge: Harvard University Press, 1986). See also the special issue of *Poetics Today* devoted to "The Female Body in Western Culture: Semiotic Perspectives," 6, nos. 1–2 (1985).

34. "Vulgívaga" is normally an adjective meaning "degrading" or "debasing." Bandeira uses it here and in several other poems as a noun signifying "prostitute" or "whore." I have left the title in the original because it suggests not only a play on "vulva" but also the Latin "vulgus" meaning "the rabble" and "vagus" meaning "wandering" or "fickle."

35. For a consideration of the language of these poems see Lúcia Helena, "Manuel Bandeira e o Lirismo de *Libertinagem,*" *Colóquio: Letras* 91 (1986):18–22.

36. See, for instance, Giovanni Pontiero, "The Expression of Irony in Manuel Bandeira's *Libertinagem,*" where he asserts (p. 846) that "the malice is gentle in the gauche utterances of the shy lover in "'Namorados.'"

37. For a provocative consideration of Bandeira's negative views on women, I am indebted to Alida Bazukis, who was kind enough to provide me with copies of her unpublished papers, "Fraternal Feminism: Sex and Aesthetics in Manuel Bandeira" and "O Aperto de Mão Fraterna: A Prostituição da Mulher na Poesia de Manuel Bandeira." An abbreviated version of the first paper was presented to the 9th Symposium on Portuguese Traditions at UCLA in April 1986.

There is no doubt that Bandeira had a complicated view of women and that many of his poems reveal a paternalistic attitude. It seems quite clear, however, that his primary goal in many of these compositions is to express a more fundamental malaise through the metaphor of heterosexual relationships.

38. This view is very different from that of Emanuel de Morais (*Manuel Bandeira,* 154). He sees the final stanza as an expression of Teresa's repentance

before God for past misdeeds; I see it as a playfully irreverent reference to intercourse between the speaker and the woman.

39. For a discussion of the Morning Star poem, see Thiago de Mello, "A Estrela da Manhã," in *Manuel Bandeira,* ed. Sônia Brayner, 211–212.

40. An extremely interesting interpretation of the poem is available in Affonso Romano de Santa'Anna, "Manuel Bandeira." The author argues (p. 203) that the poem could easily serve as "o fio condutor," or dominant motif, of the corpus as a whole.

For another discussion of the Saint Mary of Egypt theme in Bandeira's poetry, see C. Russell Reynolds, "The Santa Maria Egipcíaca Motif in Modern Brazilian Letters."

41. Another excellent example of the use of religious imagery to suggest a grim message is "Sonho de Uma Noite de Coca" (Cocaine Night's Dream), *Estrela,* 334. When the dreamer reciting the Lord's Prayer substitutes the word "dust" for "bread" ("pó" and "pão" in Portuguese), he is thinking of cocaine. However, God reminds him that he is dust (earth) and that his body will decay. The poet describes the divinity as "enternecedíssimo" ("extremely moved" by the man's request), but his words confirm the unrelenting nature of mortality. Although the individual can momentarily defy the limits that press in on him—through a drug-induced high in this case—these limits nonetheless exist.

42. Bandeira discusses a number of his Christmas poems in "Meus Poemas de Natal," *Andorinha, Andorinha,* 18–21.

43. Norma Goldstein identifies a sizable number of these in *Do Penumbrismo.*

44. The tree toad's remarks parody the ideas of the well-known Parnassian poet, Olavo Bilac (1865–1918).

45. Bandeira sought in this poem to imitate the rhythm of the French composer. "I wrote my 'Debussy,'" he notes, "in the same spirit that Schumann composed his 'Chopin'" (*Itinerário,* 71).

46. See Davi Arrigucci, Jr., "O Humilde Cotidiano de Manuel Bandeira," in *Os Pobres na Literatura Brasileira,* ed. Roberto Schwarz (São Paulo: Brasiliense, 1983), 106–122, and the same author's "O Humilde e o Sublime: Manuel Bandeira," *Folhetim* (São Paulo), No. 480 (April 20, 1980):1–12, for a discussion of everyday subjects in the poet's later work. See also Gerald Moser, "A Sensibilidade Brasileira de Manuel Bandeira," *Revista Iberoamericana* 20, no. 40 (1955): 323–333.

47. Bandeira comments on an initial version of this poem in "Gosmilhos da Pensão," *Andorinha, Andorinha,* 9–10. See also Joaquim-Francisco Coelho, "M.B. e a História dos 'Gosmilhos,'" *O Estado de São Paulo,* 7 November 1970.

48. For an analysis of this poem, see Otto Maria Carpeaux, "Ensaio de Exegese de um Poema de Manuel Bandeira," in *Manuel Bandeira,* ed. Sônia Brayner, 198–206.

49. Lêdo Ivo examines this poem in his *O Preto no Branco* (Rio de Janeiro: São José Editora, 1955).

50. The poet describes the Rua do Curvelo, the locale that inspired this poem, in *Itinerário*, 104.

51. The line "Down with purists!" ("Abaixo os puristas") originally read "Abaixo a *Revista da Língua Portuguesa*" ("Down with the *Journal of the Portuguese Language!*"), a conservative, academic publication. Bandeira changed the specific reference to make his attack broader and clearer.

For a fuller consideration of the poem, see David William Foster, "Manuel Bandeira's 'Poética.'"

52. Fernando Goés discusses the poem in "Sacha e o Poeta" in his *O Espelho Infiel: Estudos e Notas de Literatura* (São Paulo: Conselho Estadual de Cultura, Commissão de Literatura, 1966), 145–148. Bandeira describes the little girl who inspired it in "Anatomia de um Poema," *Andorinha, Andorinha*, 253.

53. This poem was based on a photograph in a book that Bandeira and his fellow poet, Augusto Frederico Schmidt, discovered in an expedition to Livraria Católica, a Rio bookshop. Schmidt proposed that each write a poem about the dead girl, Jacqueline.

54. The dictionary definition of "mirabolante," the adjective Bandeira uses to describe the musician's horse, is "showy," "gaudy," "ridiculously pompous." Because, however, the poet expressed enthusiasm for the English translation "dazzling" in this instance (see *Itinerário*, 94), I have employed the term.

55. For an early (favorable) critical reaction to the book, see João Ribeiro, "A Cinza das Horas," in *Manuel Bandeira*, ed. Sônia Brayner, 185–188. See also Joaquim-Francisco Coelho, "Uma (Re)visão de *A Cinza das Horas*," *Suplemento Literário de Minas Gerais* (3 June 1979):609.

56. The lines are from Mário de Andrade's *Paulicéia Desvairada*, available in English as *Hallucinated City*, trans. Jack E. Tomlins (Nashville: Vanderbilt University Press, 1968).

57. Bandeira's comments on the poem's genesis are transcribed in Edson Nery da Fonseca, "Carta Inédita a Edson Nery da Fonseca," *Colóquio: Letras* 91 (1986):23–25.

58. Bandeira discusses this poem in his "Rosa em Três Tempos," *Andorinha, Andorinha*, 317–321.

59. *Itinerário*, 86.

60. Ibid., 62–63.

Translator's Note

The poems that appear here represent approximately two-thirds of those included in Bandeira's principal collections published between 1930 and 1966.[1] A sampling of the early work prefaces these compositions. Because my primary purpose is to make Bandeira available to readers largely unfamiliar with his poetry, I have tried to remain faithful to the sense of the Portuguese originals while creating new rhythms and, sometimes, rhymes in English. Music—whether that of popular speech or of fixed verse forms—is the keystone of the corpus. "Just as I like [my poems] to be set to music," Bandeira says on one occasion, "so I like to be translated (at heart it is almost the same thing, isn't it?)"[2]

I have chosen texts that seemed to promise a viable English equivalent. The desire to provide the reader with the most comprehensive vision possible led me to include a wide range of poems. Some are clearly of greater literary value than others; all, nevertheless, cast light on the corpus as a whole. I myself find "Irene no Céu" (Irene in Heaven) embarrassing, "Unidade" (Union) florid, and the celebrated "A Última Canção do Beco" (Parting Song of the Alley) uncomfortably sentimental. But these texts represent important aspects of Bandeira. Moreover, not all readers will share my reaction to them.

The poet's heavy reliance on sound patterns has forced the omission of a small but significant number of his best-known compositions. "Os Sinos" (The Bells) and "Berimbau" (Berimbau, a musical instrument used by samba bands) both depend so intimately on onomatopoeia and paronomasia that they are virtually untranslatable. A good percentage of the early poems and a smaller number of later compositions employing fixed verse forms, above all, sonnets, also proved extremely difficult to translate. Some—"Peregrinação (Pilgrimage), for example—were possible to recreate as unrhymed, fourteen-line poems. Others, such as the well-known "Soneto Italiano" (Italian Sonnet), "Soneto Inglês n. 1" (English Sonnet, Number One) and "Soneto Inglês n. 2" (English Sonnet, Number Two), were not.

I was also forced to exclude a number of concrete poems and compositions involving wordplays with proper names.

Various poems that appear here have lost one or another of the dimensions they possess in the original. Wordplays effective in Portuguese are often impossible in English. "Tempo-Será," for instance, is the name for the children's game of hide-and-seek, but it also means "Time-Will-Be." "A Indesejada das Gentes" in "Consoada" (Late Supper) means "The Undesired [Female] One of the People," an invented term whose peculiarly familiar quality cannot be fully conveyed by "The Uninvited One." In a similar manner, the English version loses the alternation between "saber" (to know something) and "conhecer" (to know a person) in "A Filha do Rei" (The King's Daughter). Yet another good example of essentially untranslatable elements occurs in "O Major" (The Major), where an army bugler offers "o toque de silêncio" (an ironic "touch of silence" in Portuguese but simply "Taps" in English) at the "boca," or mouth, of the grave.

Not just the sense but the music of the Portuguese may be irrevocably altered in translation. The sonorous "boi" (pronounced "boy") that creates such a powerful refrain in "Boi Morto" (Dead Ox) becomes the disappointingly flat "ox." The substitution of "wild dove" for the native "juriti-pepena" in "Letra para Heitor dos Prazeres" (Lyrics for Heitor dos Prazeres) mutes the poem's poignant force. The subtle rhyme in "Presepe" (Manger Scene) which partially offsets the poem's extreme pessimism does not come across in English. The contrast between the first, unrhymed stanza of "Céu" (Sky) and the double rhyme of the second does not appear in the translation, which substitutes a single rhyme in both stanzas.

In addition, the echoes of children's rhymes, popular songs, and nonsense verses so important to poems like "Rondó do Capitão" (The Captain's Rondeau), "Canção de Muitas Marias" (Song of Many Marias), and "Tema e Voltas" (Theme and Variations) are less pronounced because less familiar in English. I have occasionally added or subtracted lines—see, for instance, "Pardalzinho" (Little Sparrow)—in attempting to follow the poet's dictum that the translator should identify and then strive to recreate the most important aspect of the poem.[3]

Bandeira sometimes teeters on the brink of bathos or self-pity in Portuguese but is far more apt to overstep the line in translation. He considered English the most poetic of the languages with which he was familiar ("the frankest tenderness never becomes cloying").[4] But the pungent, elusive tenderness that is a hallmark of the corpus does not always come across in "the gymnastics of translation."[5]

The use of the diminutive ("inho" or "inha"), for example, loses its sensation of affectionate proximity when translated literally as "small" or "little." The references to religious figures that sound fresh and natural in the original often become strained or stilted in translation. The everyday "Nossa!" (the "Our" of "Our Lady") is an excellent example. Although "Virgin Mary!" sounds a little better, it has different connotations than its Portuguese equivalent. (I have therefore substituted "Lord!" for "Nossa!" in the "Rondó dos Cavalinhos" [Rondeau of the Little Horses].) Even more difficult to render are terms allied with Afro-Brazilian religions: the "saravá" used to greet the gods in "Dona Janaína," for example, or "macumba" (an extremely complex and varied religious system) in "Macumba de Pai Zusé" (Voodoo at Pai Zusé's).

Bandeira's attempts to give certain poems an everyday flavor through the imitation of popular speech patterns poses a similar problem. Rather than attempting to render his "pra" for "para" as "fur"instead of "for," I have on most occasions sought to create a general conversational tone. Place-names appear in English when the literal translation enhances the colloquial and often humorous quality of the original but remain in Portuguese when they do not have the desired effect. Moreover, I have adapted my translation to the circumstances. On one occasion, for instance, "Pouso Alto" appears as "Lofty Perch"; on another, as "Mountain Rest." Depending on the rhythmic necessities of the poem in question, "Maria" may be "Maria" "Mary," or "Marie."

English-speaking readers will appreciate Bandeira's skillful evocation of everyday customs, local landmarks, and folkways. But these elements often lose the everyday quality they possess in Portuguese and may even take on an exotic connotation in English. The comparison of a woman's sex to a tamarind in "Água-Forte" (Aqua Fortis), for instance, suggests one thing to readers who have a tree of this type in their backyard and another to those for whom the fruit is only a lovely name. Likewise, the neighborhoods the poet cites in "Tragédia Brasileira" (Brazilian Tragedy), actual places for the individual familiar with Rio de Janeiro, remain an amusing bit of wordplay for the nonresident.

Similarly, non-Brazilian readers can easily imagine the three soap wrapper muses in "Balada das Três Mulheres do Sabonete Araxá (Ballad of the Three Women on the Araxá Soap Wrapper). They, however, will not have taken a bath with the soap or remember the pictures, tucked inside the package, that children used to trade much like baseball cards. Furthermore, while they may recognize the echoes of Shakespeare, Spenser, and Dante in this poem, most are unlikely to detect the presence of Portuguese and Brazilian authors such as Olavo Bilac, Castro Alves, Luís Delfino, and Eugênio de Castro.

I have used end notes to explain such allusions to Brazilian and Portuguese literature, art, and music and to more general aspects of Brazilian life and culture—the bonfires and fire balloons traditionally used to celebrate the summer solstice, for example. As none of the texts in this collection is incomprehensible without notes, I have preferred to provide this information by poem heading in a separate section rather than to introduce numbers or asterisks into the actual texts. As certain features of these poems have already been explained in the introduction and accompanying notes, I have not repeated this material.

Critics have emphasized time and again the persistently regional and national quality of Bandeira's poetry. And yet, despite his roots in daily life and language, Bandeira remains gratifyingly accessible to the non-Portuguese-speaking reader. Complex in their apparent simplicity, the poems document the multifaceted and often contradictory passage from one literary and historical moment to another. Their unmistakably Brazilian rhythms, vocabulary, and cultural content give them an appealing particularity; the larger questions they pose make them universal.

NOTES

1. The collected works contain a number of occasional poems and poems written for particular persons brought together under the rubric "Outros Poemas" (Other Poems). Although some of these compositions are interesting, I have chosen to restrict myself to the body of Bandeira's work. The fact that he moved a number of compositions originally included in his principal volumes to the "Other Poems" section in the definitive edition of his collected work suggests that he considered them to be of secondary importance.

2. *Itinerário*, 94.

3. Ibid., 94.

4. Ibid., 120.

5. The term "a ginástica da tradução" is Bandeira's. See ibid., 101.

A CINZA DAS HORAS
ASH OF THE HOURS
1917

EPÍGRAFE

Sou bem-nascido. Menino,
Fui, como os demais, feliz.
Depois, veio o mau destino
E fez de mim o que quis.

Veio o mau gênio da vida,
Rompeu em meu coração,
Levou tudo de vencida,
Rugiu como um furacão,

Turbou, partiu, abateu,
Queimou sem razão nem dó—
Ah, que dor!
                    Magoado e só,
—Só!—meu coração ardeu.

Ardeu em gritos dementes
Na sua paixão sombria . . .
E dessas horas ardentes
Ficou esta cinza fria.

—Esta pouca cinza fria . . .

POEMETO ERÓTICO

Teu corpo claro e perfeito,
— Teu corpo de maravilha,
Quero possuí-lo no leito
Estreito da redondilha . . .

Teu corpo é tudo o que cheira . . .
Rosa . . . flor de laranjeira . . .

EPIGRAPH

I'm from a good home. A child,
I was like all the rest.
Until, that is, that fate stormed in
and put me to its test.

One of life's evil moods came on.
It burst within my breast,
then howling like a cyclone,
swept off all I possessed.

It shook me, split me, razed me,
burned without reason or pity—what pain!
Anguished and alone,

—alone!—my heart raged,

raged in its dark passion,
in howling grief insane . . .
And of those fiery hours
just these cold ashes remain.

—This handful of cold ashes . . .

LITTLE EROTIC POEM

Your clear and perfect body
so marvelous and fine,
I want to possess your body
in the narrow bed of my rhyme.

Your body is all fragrance . . .
Rose and orange blossom . . .

Teu corpo, branco e macio,
É como um véu de noivado . . .

Teu corpo é pomo doirado . . .

Rosal queimado do estio,
Desfalecido em perfume . . .

Teu corpo é a brasa do lume . . .

Teu corpo é chama e flameja
Como à tarde os horizontes . . .

É puro como nas fontes
A água clara que serpeja,
Que em cantigas se derrama . . .

Volúpia da água e da chama . . .

A todo o momento o vejo . . .
Teu corpo . . . única ilha
No oceano do meu desejo . . .

Teu corpo é tudo o que brilha,
Teu corpo é tudo o que cheira . . .
Rosa, flor de laranjeira . . .

BODA ESPIRITUAL

Tu não estás comigo em momentos escassos:
No pensamento meu, amor, tu vives nua
— Toda nua, pudica e bela, nos meus braços.

O teu ombro no meu, ávido, se insinua.
Pende a tua cabeça. Eu amacio-a . . . Afago-a . . .
Ah, como a minha mão treme . . . Como ela é tua . . .

Your body, white and smooth,
is like a wedding veil . . .

Your body is a golden fruit . . .

Parched rosebush of summer
drooping in its own perfume . . .

Your body is the fire's live embers . . .

Your body is a flame that blazes
like the early evening skies . . .

It is pure like the clear water
of the fountain that spirals,
pouring out in song . . .

Carnal passion of the water and the flame . . .

I see it constantly before me
Your body . . . the sole island
in the ocean of my desire . . .

Your body is all radiance . . .
Your body is all fragrance . . .
Rose and orange blossom . . .

SPIRITUAL WEDDING

You are not with me in fleeting moments
but live, my love, within my mind
—Chaste, beautiful and wholly nude within my arms.

Your shoulder eagerly presses ever closer against mine.
You bow your head. I stroke, caress it.
How my hand trembles . . . How it has become yours . . .

Põe no teu rosto o gozo uma expressão de mágoa.
O teu corpo crispado alucina. De escorço
O vejo estremecer como uma sombra n'água.

Gemes quase a chorar. Suplicas com esforço.
E para amortecer teu ardente desejo
Estendo longamente a mão pelo teu dorso . . .

Tua boca sem voz implora em um arquejo.
Eu te estreito cada vez mais, e espio absorto
A maravilha astral dessa nudez sem pejo . . .

E te amo como se ama um passarinho morto.

Pleasure gives your face an expression of sorrow.
Your tensed body fills me with desire. From this angle
I see it shudder like a shadow on the water.

Your moan is almost a sob. You plead insistently
and to quench your feverish desire
I slowly trail my hand along your back . . .

Wordless, you implore me in a gasp.
I hold you closer, closer, and spellbound, observe
the starlike marvel of this nudity that knows no shame . . .

And I love you as one loves a small and lifeless bird.

CARNAVAL
CARNIVAL
1919

OS SAPOS

Enfunando os papos,
Saem da penumbra,
Aos pulos, os sapos.
A luz os deslumbra.

Em ronco que aterra,
Berra o sapo-boi:
- "Meu pai foi à guerra!"
- "Não foi!" — "Foi!" — "Não foi!".

O sapo-tanoeiro,
Parnasiano aguado,
Diz: — "Meu cancioneiro
É bem martelado.

Vede como primo
Em comer os hiatos!
Que arte! E nunca rimo
Os termos cognatos.

O meu verso é bom
Frumento sem joio.
Faço rimas com
Consoantes de apoio.

Vai por cinqüenta anos
Que lhes dei a norma:
Reduzi sem danos
A formas a forma.

Clame a saparia
Em críticas céticas:
Não há mais poesia,
Mas há artes poéticas . . . "

THE TOADS

Puffing out their necks,
the toads leap into sight.
Emerging from the shadows,
they are dazzled by the light.

With startling hoarseness
the bull-toad roars
—"My father went to war!"
—"He didn't!"—"He did!"—"He didn't!"

A washed-up Parnassian,
the tree toad repeats—
"My repertoire possesses
a well-hammered beat.

Look at how I excel
at swallowing the hiatus!
What artistic skill! And still
I never ever rhyme a cognate.

My verses are wheat
without chaff since all the time
I fashion verses
with extra syllables for rhymes.

Nearly fifty years ago
I set up my norms:
reducing without harm
forms into form.

The toad-chorus
cynically retorts:
"Poetry is dead.
There are just poetic arts . . . "

Urra o sapo-boi:
— "Meu pai foi rei" — "Foi!"
— "Não foi!" — "Foi!" — "Não foi!".

Brada em um assomo
O sapo-tanoeiro:
— "A grande arte é como
Lavor de joalheiro.

Ou bem de estatuário.
Tudo quanto é belo,
Tudo quanto é vário,
Canta no martelo."

Outros, sapos-pipas
Um mal em si cabe),
Falam pelas tripas:
— "Sei!" — "Não sabe!" — "Sabe!".

Longe dessa grita,
Lá onde mais densa
A noite infinita
Verte a sombra imensa;

Lá, fugido ao mundo,
Sem glória, sem fé,
No perau profundo
E solitário, é

Que soluças tu,
Transido de frio,
Sapo-cururu
Da beira do rio . . .

The bull-toad roars:
—"My father was king"—"He was!"
—"Wasn't!"—"Was!"—"Wasn't!"

The tree toad brays,
enormously irked.
—"Great art is like
the jeweler's work.

Or the sculptor's craft.
Beat out in measured verse
all that is beautiful
and most diverse."

Others, Surinam toads
(one seems ready to explode)
talk through their guts:
—"I know!"—"You don't!"—"Oh he does so!"

Far from their shouts
where the night so intense
pours out its shadow
dark and immense;

There, hidden to the world
with no glory, no creed,
tucked away in a bog
so lonely and deep,

Shot through with cold,
chilled to the bone—
It's there that you weep,
small river toad . . .

VULGÍVAGA

Não posso crer que se conceba
Do amor senão o gozo físico!
O meu amante morreu bêbado,
E meu marido morreu tísico!

Não sei entre que astutos dedos
Deixei a rosa da inocência.
Antes da minha pubescência
Sabia todos os segredos . . .

Fui de um . . . Fui de outro . . . Este era médico
Um, poeta . . . Outro, nem sei mais!
Tive em meu leito enciclopédico
Todas as artes liberais.

Aos velhos dou o meu engulho.
Aos férvidos, o que os esfrie.
A artistas, a *coquetterie*
Que inspira . . . E aos tímidos — o orgulho.

Estes, caçôo-os e depeno-os:
A canga fez-se para o boi . . .
Meu claro ventre nunca foi
De sonhadores e de ingênuos!

E todavia se o primeiro
Que encontro, fere toda a lira,
Amanso. Tudo se me tira.
Dou tudo. E mesmo . . . dou dinheiro . . .

Se bate, então como o estremeço!
Oh, a volúpia da pancada!
Dar-me entre lágrimas, quebrada
Do seu colérico arremesso . . .

VULGÍVAGA

I can't believe that anyone could think of love
as anything but carnal pleasure!
My lover died an alcoholic
and my husband a consumptive.

I don't know between what practiced fingers
I left the rose of innocence.
I knew all the secrets
before adolescence.

I belonged to one . . . another . . . this one was a doctor . . .
that a poet . . . I don't recall the rest!
I've had all the liberal arts
in my encyclopedic bed.

I lend old men my passion,
cool the feverish,
I inspire artists with my coquetry
instill pride in the timid.

Others I mock, make off with their last cent.
The yoke was made to fit the ox . . .
My luminous belly has never been the property
of innocents and dreamers.

And yet, if the first man I meet
strikes the right note,
I melt. All can be had of me.
I give all . . . yes, even money.

If he hits me, how I like him.
Oh, the pleasure of the blow!
To give myself amidst tears, broken
by his furious assault . . .

E o cio atroz se me não leva
A valhacoutos de canalhas,
É porque temo pela treva
O fio fino das navalhas . . .

Não posso crer que se conceba
Do amor senão o gozo físico!
O meu amante morreu bêbado,
E meu marido morreu tísico!

DEBUSSY

Para cá, para lá . . .
Para cá, para lá . . .
Um novelozinho de linha . . .
Para cá, para lá . . .
Para cá, para lá . . .
Oscila no ar pela mão de uma criança
(Vem e vai . . .)
Que delicadamente e quase a adormecer o balança
— Psio . . . —
Para cá, para lá . . .
Para cá e . . .
— O novelozinho caiu.

And if an animal passion doesn't drive me
to seek out scoundrels' lairs,
it's only because I fear the blade's fine edge
amidst the shadows.

I can't believe that anyone could think of love
as anything but carnal pleasure!
My lover died an alcoholic
and my husband a consumptive.

DEBUSSY

To and fro, to and fro . . .
To and fro, to and fro . . .
A little ball of string . . .
To and fro, to and fro . . .
To and fro, to and fro . . .
The ball swings (back and forth)
from the hand of a child
who, half asleep, lets it gently dangle
—Psst . . .
To and fro, to and fro . . .
To and . . .
The little ball has dropped.

O RITMO DISSOLUTO
FREED RHYTHM
1924

BALADA DE SANTA MARIA EGIPCÍACA

Santa Maria Egipcíaca seguia
Em peregrinação à terra do Senhor.

Caía o crepúsculo, e era como um triste sorriso de mártir.

Santa Maria Egipcíaca chegou
À beira de um grande rio.
Era tão longe a outra margem!
E estava junto à ribanceira,
Num barco,
Um homem de olhar duro.

Santa Maria Egipcíaca rogou:
— Leva-me ao outro lado.
Não tenho dinheiro. O Senhor te abençoe.

O homem duro fitou-a sem dó.

Caía o crepúsculo, e era como um triste sorriso de mártir.

— Não tenho dinheiro. A Senhor te abençoe.
Leva-me ao outro lado.

O homem duro escarneceu: — Não tens dinheiro,
Mulher, mas tens teu corpo. Dá-me o teu corpo, e vou levar-te.

E fez um gesto. E a santa sorriu,
Na graça divina, ao gesto que ele fez.

Santa Maria Egipcíaca despiu
O manto, e entregou ao barqueiro
A santidade da sua nudez.

BALLAD OF SAINT MARY OF EGYPT

Saint Mary of Egypt went
to the Holy Land in pilgrimage.

The twilight was falling like the sad smile of a martyr.

Saint Mary of Egypt arrived
at the bank of a great river.
The other side was so far off!
And near the shore,
a hard-eyed boatman.

Saint Mary of Egypt pleaded:
—"Take me to the other side.
I have no money. God will reward you."

The hard-eyed man stared at her without pity.

The twilight was falling like the sad smile of a martyr.

—"I have no money. God will reward you.
Take me to the other side."

The hard-eyed man scoffed: "You have no money, woman, but
     you have your body. Give me your body and I will take you."

And he made a gesture. And the saint smiled at his gesture
     in divine grace.

Saint Mary of Egypt took off her robe
and yielded to the boatman
the sanctity of her naked body.

MADRIGAL MELANCÓLICO

O que eu adoro em ti
Não é a tua beleza.
A beleza, é em nós que ela existe.
A beleza é um conceito.
E a beleza é triste.
Não é triste em si,
Mas pelo que há nela de fragilidade e de incerteza

O que eu adoro em ti,
Não é a tua inteligência.
Não é o teu espírito sutil,
Tão ágil, tão luminoso,
— Ave solta no céu matinal da montanha.
Nem é a tua ciência
Do coração dos homens e das coisas.

O que eu adoro em ti,
Não é a tua graça musical,
Sucessiva e renovada a cada momento,
Graça aérea como o teu próprio pensamento,
Graça que perturba e que satisfaz.

O que eu adoro em ti,
Não é a mãe que já perdi.
Não é a irmã que já perdi.
E meu pai.

O que eu adoro em tua natureza,
Não é o profundo instinto maternal
Em teu flanco aberto como uma ferida.
Nem a tua pureza. Nem a tua impureza.
O que eu adoro em ti — lastima-me e consola-me!
O que eu adoro em ti, é a vida.

MELANCHOLY MADRIGAL

What I adore in you
isn't your beauty.
Beauty exists within us.
Beauty is an idea.
And beauty is sad,
not sad in itself
but for what is fragile and unsure.

What I adore in you
isn't your intelligence
or your subtle spirit,
so luminous, so quick
—bird uncaged in mountain morning.
It's not your knowledge
of the heart of men and things.

What I adore in you
isn't your musical grace,
ceaseless and forever new,
airborne like your own thought,
grace which perturbs and pleases.

What I adore in you
isn't the mother I have lost.
Isn't the sister I have lost.
Or my father.

What I adore in you
isn't the mother's love
in your side opened like a wound.
It's not your purity. Not your impurity.
What I adore in you—oh pity and console me!
What I adore in you is life.

MENINOS CARVOEIROS

Os meninos carvoeiros
Passam a caminho da cidade.
— Eh, carvoero!
E vão tocando os animais com um relho enorme.

Os burros são magrinhos e velhos.
Cada um leva seis sacos de carvão de lenha.
A aniagem é toda remendada.
Os carvões caem.

(Pela boca da noite vem uma velhinha que os recolhe, dobrando-se
                                        [com um gemido.)

— Eh, carvoero!

Só mesmo estas crianças raquíticas
Vão bem com estes burrinhos descadeirados.
A madrugada ingênua parece feita para eles . . .
Pequenina, ingênua miséria!
Adoráveis carvoeirinhos que trabalhais como se brincásseis

— Eh, carvoero!

Quando voltam, vêm mordendo num pão encarvoado,
Encarapitados nas alimárias,
Apostando corrida,
Dançando, bamboleando nas cangalhas como espantalhos
                                        [desamparados!

A MATA

A mata agita-se, revoluteia, contorce-se toda e sacode-se!
A mata hoje tem alguma coisa para dizer.
E ulula, e contorce-se toda, como a atriz de uma pantomima
                                        [trágica.

LITTLE COALMEN

The little coal peddlers
pass by on their way into town.
—Hey there, coal'mun!
And they prod their animals with an enormous whip.

The little donkeys are old and scrawny.
Each carries six sacks of coal.
The burlap is patched together.
The coal slips out the holes.

(At twilight an old lady gathers up the pieces with a moan.)

—Hey there, coal'mun!

These painfully thin children
are a good match for the hipshot donkeys.
The ingenuous dawn seems made for them.
Small, ingenuous misery!
Lovable little peddlers who work as if at play!

—Hey there, coal'mun!

On their return they gnaw a crust of grimy bread,
astride their beasts,
racing each other home,
dancing, lurching, in the saddle
like abandoned scarecrows!

THE WOODS

The woods toss, whirl, lurch, writhe.
The woods today have something on their mind.
And they howl and flail about like an actress in a tragic
    pantomime.

Cada galho rebelado
Inculca a mesma perdida ânsia.
Todos eles sabem o mesmo segredo pânico.
Ou então — é que pedem desesperadamente a mesma instante
[coisa.

Que saberá a mata? Que pedirá a mata?
Pedirá água?
Mas a água despenhou-se há pouco, fustigando-a, escorraçando-a,
[saciando-a como aos alarves.
Pedirá o fogo para a purificação das necroses milenárias?
Ou não pede nada, e quer falar e não pode?
Terá surpreendido o segredo da terra pelos ouvidos finíssimos das
[suas raízes?
A mata agita-se, revoluteia, contorce-se toda e sacode-se!
A mata está hoje como uma multidão em delírio coletivo.

Só uma touça de bambus, à parte,
Balouça levemente . . . levemente . . . levemente . . .
E parece sorrir do delírio geral.

NOITE MORTA

Noite morta.
Junto ao poste de iluminação
Os sapos engolem mosquitos.

Ninguém passa na estrada.
Nem um bêbado.

No entanto há seguramente por ela uma procissão de sombras.
Sombras de todos os que passaram.
Os que ainda vivem e os que já morreram.

Each rebel branch
betrays the same desperate fear.
All know the same secret panic.
Or perhaps they are all frantically seeking the same thing.

What could the woods know? What could they want?
Water, perhaps?
But the rains came flooding down just a short time ago, whipping
    them, uprooting them, sating their gluttonous thirst.
Could they be seeking fire to purify an age-old rot?
Or do they seek nothing? Do they merely want to speak and can't?
Could they have overheard the earth's secret through their
    roots' oh-so-tender ears?
The woods toss, whirl, lurch, writhe.
The woods today are like a frenzied mob.

Only a lone clump of bamboo over to one side
sways to and fro, to and fro
as if smiling at the general madness.

DEAD OF NIGHT

Dead of night.
Beside the light post
toads gulp down mosquitoes.

No one passes on the road.
Not even a drunk.

Still, there is most certainly a procession of shadows.
Shadows of everyone who ever passed here,
those still living, those already dead.

O córrego chora.
A voz da noite . . .

(Não desta noite, mas de outra maior.)

NA RUA DO SABÃO

Cai cai balão
Cai cai balão
Na Rua do Sabão!

O que custou arranjar aquele balãozinho de papel!
Quem fez foi o filho da lavadeira.
Um que trabalha na composição do jornal e tosse muito.
Comprou o papel de seda, cortou-o com amor, compôs os gomos
                                                [oblongos . . .
Depois ajustou o morrão de pez ao bocal de arame.

Ei-lo agora que sobe — pequena coisa tocante na escuridão do céu.

Levou tempo para criar fôlego.
Bambeava, tremia todo e mudava de cor.
A molecada da Rua do Sabão
Gritava com maldade:
Cai cai balão!

Subitamente, porém, entesou, enfunou-se e arrancou das mãos que
                                                [o tenteavam.
E foi subindo . . .
                para longe . . .
                        serenamente . . .
Como se o enchesse o soprinho tísico do José.

Cai cai balão!

The brook weeps.
The voice of the night . . .

(Not of this night, but of another, larger.)

SOAP STREET

Down, down, balloon
Down, down, balloon
Go down in town,
go down on Soap Street!

What a job to put together that little paper fire balloon!
It was the washerwoman's son—
the one who works at the typesetter
and who is always coughing—
He bought tissue paper, cut it lovingly,
    joined the narrow sections,
then attached the tarred wick to the wire mouthpiece.

Look at it now as it climbs upward—so small, so moving
    in the sky's darkness.

It took a long time to get its wind.
It swayed and shook, changed color.
The street urchins
yelled maliciously
Down, down balloon!

Suddenly, however, it stiffened, swelled, pulled loose.

And it went on climbing . . .
                        a long way . . .
                                        very calmly . . .
as if buoyed by José's consumptive breath.

Down, down balloon!

A molecada salteou-o com atiradeiras
       assobios
       apupos
       pedradas.
Cai cai balão!

Um senhor advertiu que os balões são proibidos pelas posturas
                          [municipais.

Ele foi subindo . . .
         muito serenamente . . .
               para muito longe . . .

Não caiu na Rua do Sabão.
Caiu muito longe . . . Caiu no mar — nas águas puras do mar
                          [alto.

BALÕEZINHOS

Na feira-livre do arrabaldezinho
Um homem loquaz apregoa balõezinhos de cor:
— "O melhor divertimento para as crianças!"
Em redor dele há um ajuntamento de menininhos pobres,
Fitando com olhos muito redondos os grandes balõezinhos muito
                          [redondos.

No entanto a feira burburinha.
Vão chegando as burguesinhas pobres,
E as criadas das burguesinhas ricas,
E mulheres do povo, e as lavadeiras da redondeza.

Nas bancas de peixe,
Nas barranquinhas de cereais,
Junto às cestas de hortaliças
O tostão é regateado com acrimônia.

The urchins attacked with slingshots
      hoots
      jeers
      stones.
Down, down balloon!

A gentleman warned that city ordinance prohibits such balloons.

It continued to climb . . .
                  very calmly . . .
                                very far . . .

It didn't fall on Soap Street.
It fell far away . . . It fell into the sea—the clear waters
      of the high sea.

BALLOONS

In the open-air market on the fringes of town
a chatterbox peddler hawks his brightly colored balloons:
—"A most excellent pastime for children!"
Around him a crowd of poor children
fasten round eyes on the great round balloons.

Meanwhile the market bubbles with activity.
The more modest ladies-of-the-house arrive
together with the richer ladies' maids,
the workers' wives and local washerwomen.

In the fish stands,
at the grain stalls,
beside the huge baskets full of greens,
they haggle over pennies.

Os meninos pobres não vêem as ervilhas tenras,
Os tomatinhos vermelhos,
Nem as frutas,
Nem nada.

Sente-se bem que para eles ali na feira os balõezinhos de cor são a
            [única mercadoria útil e verdadeiramente indispensável.

O vendedor infatigável apregoa:
— "O melhor divertimento para as crianças!"
E em torno do homem loquaz os menininhos pobres fazem um
            [círculo inamovível de desejo e espanto.

The poor children don't notice the tender new peas,
the cherry tomatoes,
or the fruit.
They notice nothing.

Clearly, for them the bright balloons are the only thing
that counts, that really matters.

The tireless vendor goes on:
—"A most excellent pastime for children!"
And around the chatterbox man the poor children form
a fixed circle of desire and wonder.

LIBERTINAGEM
LIBERTINISM
1930

O ANJO DA GUARDA

Quando minha irmã morreu,
(Devia ter sido assim)
Um anjo moreno, violento e bom, — brasileiro

Veio ficar ao pé de mim.
O meu anjo da guarda sorriu
E voltou para junto do Senhor.

MULHERES

Como as mulheres são lindas!
Inútil pensar que é do vestído . . .
E depois não há só as bonitas:
Há também as simpáticas.
E as feias, certas feias em cujos olhos vejo isto:

Uma menininha que é batida e pisada e nunca sai da cozinha

Como deve ser bom gostar de uma feia!
O meu amor porém não tem bondade alguma.
É fraco! fraco!
Meu Deus, eu amo como as criancinhas . . .

És linda como uma história da carochinha . . .
E eu preciso de ti como precisava de mamãe e papai
(No tempo em que pensava que os ladrões moravam no morro
                    [atrás de casa e tinham cara de pau).

GUARDIAN ANGEL

When my sister died
(It must have been this way)
An angel, dark, impetuous and kind—Brazilian

came to stand beside me.
My guardian angel smiled
and returned to the side of the Lord.

WOMEN

How lovely women are!
Useless to say they're pretty because of a pretty dress
—besides, there are not only those with looks
but those you simply can't help liking.
There are also homely women, certainly homely women in whose
    eyes I see
a little girl who is beaten and abused and who never leaves
    the kitchen.

How good it must be to love a homely woman!
But my loving doesn't have a shred of kindness . . .
It's weak. Weak!
My God, I love like a little kid . . .

You're as pretty as a fairy tale . . .
And I need you like I needed Mommy and Daddy
(In those days when I thought thieves lived on the hill behind our
    house and had wooden faces.)

PENSÃO FAMILIAR

Jardim da pensãozinha burguesa.
Gatos espapaçados ao sol.
A tiririca sitia os canteiros chatos.
O sol acaba de crestar as boninas que murcharam.
Os girassóis
                    amarelo!
                                    resistem.
E as dálias, rechonchudas, plebéias, dominicais.

Um gatinho faz pipi.
Com gestos de garçom de restaurant-Palace
Encobre cuidadosamente a mijadinha.
Sai vibrando com elegância a patinha direita:
— É a única criatura fina na pensãozinha burguesa.

CAMELÔS

Abençoado seja o camelô dos brinquedos de tostão:
O que vende balõezinhos de cor
O macaquinho que trepa no coqueiro
O cachorrinho que bate com o rabo
Os homenzinhos que jogam box
A pererereca verde que de repente dá um pulo que engraçado
E as canetinhas-tinteiro que jamais escreverão coisa alguma
Alegria das calçadas

Uns falam pelos cotovelos:
— "O cavalheiro chega em casa e diz: Meu filho, vai buscar
   um pedaço de banana para eu acender o charuto. Natu-
   ralmente o menino pensará: Papai está malu . . . "

Outros, coitados, têm a língua atada.

TWO-STAR HOTEL

Garden of the little two-star resident hotel.
Cats grown lazy in the sun.
The sedge plant lays siege to the monotonous flower beds.
The sun singes the already withered four o'clocks
while the sunflowers
                              so yellow!
                                        resist.
And the dahlias—plump, plebeian, in their Sunday best.

A kitten takes a piss.
With the flourish of a waiter in the Palace
He covers the small puddle carefully
and goes off, elegantly shaking his right paw
—the only superior creature in the little two-star hotel.

STREET VENDORS

Blessed be the vendors of penny toys
who hawk brightly colored balloons,
along with the wooden monkey jumping up the palm tree,
the little dog wagging his tail,
the green frog who gives a sudden leap—what fun!—
and the fountain pens that will never write a blessed word.
They are the life of the sidewalks . . .

Some talk a blue streak:
—"The gentleman arrives home and says, "Son, go get a piece
    of banana so I can light my cigar." Of course the kid
    immediately thinks, "Dad's really lost his marb . . . "

Others, poor things, are tongue-tied.

Todos porém sabem mexer nos cordéis com o tino ingênuo de
[demiurgos de inutilidades.
E ensinam no tumulto das ruas os mitos heróicos da meninice . . .
E dão aos homens que passam preocupados ou tristes uma lição de
[infância.

O CACTO

Aquele cacto lembrava os gestos desesperados da estatuária:
Laocoonte constrangido pelas serpentes,
Ugolino e os filhos esfaimados.
Evocava também o seco Nordeste, carnaubais, caatingas . . .
Era enorme, mesmo para esta terra de feracidades excepcionais.

Um dia um tufão furibundo abateu-o pela raiz.
O cacto tombou atravessado na rua,
Quebrou os beirais do casario fronteiro,
Impediu o trânsito de bondes, automóveis, carroças,
Arrebentou os cabos elétricos e durante vinte e quatro horas privou
[a cidade de iluminação e energia:

— Era belo, áspero, intratável.

PNEUMOTÓRAX

Febre, hemoptise, dispnéia e suores noturnos.
A vida inteira que podia ter sido e que não foi.
Tosse, tosse, tosse.

Mandou chamar o médico:
— Diga trinta e três.
— Trinta e três . . . trinta e três . . . trinta e três . . .
— Respire.

And yet, they still know how to work the strings with the artless
    skill of demigods of trifles.
And they teach the old heroic myths of children amidst the tumult
    of the street
and give the sad or worried passersby a lesson in childhood.

THE CACTUS

That cactus recalled the frantic gestures of statues:
Laocoön fettered by serpents,
Ugolino and his famished sons.
It also suggested the parched Northeast, the palm trees,
    scrub grass . . .
It was enormous, even for this exceptionally luxuriant land.

One day it was uprooted by a raging gale.
The cactus fell across the street
smashing the eaves of houses across the way,
blocking trolleys, wagons, cars,
snapping power lines, robbing the city for a whole day of light and
    power.

—It was beautiful, harsh, unyielding.

PNEUMOTHORAX

Fever, bloody coughing, labored breathing and night sweats.
The whole life that could have been and wasn't.
Cough, cough, cough.

He sent for the doctor:
—"Cough for me, please."
—"Ahem . . . Ahem . . . Ahem . . . "
"Now breathe."

— O senhor tem uma escavação no pulmão esquerdo e o pulmão
[direito infiltrado.
— Então, doutor, não é possível tentar o pneumotórax?
— Não. A única coisa a fazer é tocar um tango argentino.

COMENTÁRIO MUSICAL

O meu quarto de dormir a cavaleiro da entrada da barra.
Entram por ele dentro
Os ares oceânicos,
Maresias atlânticas:
São Paulo de Luanda, Figueira da Foz, praias gaélicas da
[Irlanda . . .

O comentário musical da paisagem só podia ser o sussurro
[sinfônico da vida civil.

No entanto o que ouço neste momento é um silvo agudo de
[sagüim:
Minha vizinha de baixo comprou um sagüim.

POÉTICA

Estou farto do lirismo comedido
Do lirismo bem comportado
Do lirismo funcionário público com livro de ponto expedien-
te protocolo e manifestações de apreço ao sr. diretor.

Estou farto do lirismo que pára e vai averiguar no dicioná-
rio o cunho vernáculo de um vocábulo

—"You have a hole in the left lung and fluid in the right."
—"So then, doctor, isn't it possible to attempt a pneumothorax?"
—"No. The only thing to do is strike up an Argentine tango."

MUSICAL COMMENTARY

My bedroom above the harbor.
Through it enter
ocean winds,
salt breezes from the Atlantic—
São Paulo de Luanda, Figueira da Foz, the Gaelic sands
    of Ireland . . .

The musical gloss on this scene could only be the symphonic
    murmur of daily life.

And yet what I am hearing is a little monkey's shrill hiss.

(My downstairs neighbor has just bought a pet monkey.)

POETICS

I'm sick of cautious lyricism
of well-behaved lyricism
of a civil servant lyricism complete with time card office hours
    set procedures and expressions of esteem for Mr. Boss, Sir.

I'm sick of the lyricism that has to stop in midstream to look up
    the precise meaning of a word.

Abaixo os puristas
Todas as palavras sobretudo os barbarismos universais
Todas as construções sobretudo as sintaxes de exceção
Todos os ritmos sobretudo os inumeráveis

Estou farto do lirismo namorador
Político
Raquítico
Sifilítico
De todo lirismo que capitula ao que quer que seja fora de si
[mesmo.

De resto não é lirismo
Será contabilidade tabela de co-senos secretário do amante
    exemplar com cem modelos de cartas e as diferentes ma-
    neiras de agradar às mulheres, etc.

Quero antes o lirismo dos loucos
O lirismo dos bêbados
O lirismo difícil e pungente dos bêbados
O lirismo dos clowns de Shakespeare

— Não quero mais saber do lirismo que não é libertação.

BONHEUR LYRIQUE

Cœur de phtisique
O mon cœur lyrique
Ton bonheur ne peut pas être comme celui des autres

Il faut que tu te fabriques
Un bonheur unique
Un bonheur qui soit comme le piteux lustucru en chiffon d'une
                                         [enfant pauvre
—Fait par elle-même.

Down with purists!
Up with
all words, especially those that everyone gets wrong
all constructions, above all exceptions to the rule
all rhythms, above all those that can't be counted.

I'm sick of philandering lyricism—
political
raquitical
syphilitical
—of all lyricism that gives in to any outside force.

Besides, all this other business isn't lyricism—
It's accounting cosine tables a handbook for the model lover
    with a hundred form letters and different ways of pleasing
    women, etc.

I prefer the lyricism of madmen
the lyricism of drunks
the difficult and bitter lyricism of the drunk
the lyricism of Shakespeare's clowns

I want nothing more of lyricism that isn't liberation.

BONHEUR LYRIQUE

Consumptive heart,
oh my lyric heart,
your joy can't be like that of others.

You must create
a joy that's your own
a joy like the poor child's pitiful fantasy in chiffon

that she creates all alone.

PORQUINHO-DA-ÍNDIA

Quando eu tinha seis anos
Ganhei um porquinho-da-índia.
Que dor de coração me dava
Porque o bichinho só queria estar debaixo do fogão!
Levava ele prà sala
Pra os lugares mais bonitos mais limpinhos
Ele não gostava:
Queria era estar debaixo do fogão,
Não fazia caso nenhum das minhas ternurinhas . . .

— O meu porquinho-da-índia foi a minha primeira namorada.

EVOCAÇÃO DO RECIFE

Recife
Não a Veneza americana
Não a Mauritsstad dos armadores das Índias Ocidentais

Não o Recife dos Mascates
Nem mesmo a Recife que aprendi a amar depois —
    Recife das revoluções libertárias
Mas o Recife sem história nem literatura
Recife sem mais nada
Recife da minha infância

A Rua da União onde eu brincava de chicote-queimado e partia as
                            [vidraças da casa de dona Aninha Viegas
Totônio Rodrigues era muito velho e botava o pincenê na ponta do
                                                        [nariz
Depois do jantar as famílias tomavam a calçada com cadeiras,
                            [mexericos, namoros, risadas
A gente brincava no meio da rua
Os meninos gritavam:

GUINEA PIG

When I was six years old
they gave me a guinea pig.
What heartache it caused me—
all the little creature wanted was to hide out under the stove!
I carried it to the living room,
to the prettiest and best-kept corners of the house
but it didn't like them.
All it wanted was to hide out under the stove.
It didn't pay my affectionate gestures the slightest notice.

—My guinea pig was my first girlfriend.

EVOCATION OF RECIFE

Recife
Not the American Venice,
not the Mauritsstad of the merchants of the Dutch East India
    Company
not the Recife of Portuguese peddlers
not even the Recife I later learned to love—
    the Recife of freedom-seeking revolutions
but a Recife without history or literature
Recife plain and simple
the Recife of my childhood

Union Street where I played crack-the-whip and broke
    Dona Aninha Viegas's windows
Totônio Rodrigues was very old and wore his pince-nez on the tip
    of his nose
After dinner the families took their chairs out on the sidewalk,
    —gossip, flirting, laughter
We children played in the street
The boys shouted:

Coelho sai!
Não sai!

À distância as vozes macias das meninas politonavam:

Roseira dá-me uma rosa
Craveiro dá-me um botão

(Dessas rosas muita rosa
Terá morrido em botão . . .)

De repente
nos longes da noite
um sino

Uma pessoa grande dizia:
Fogo em Santo Antônio!
Outra contrariava: São José!
Totônio Rodrigues achava sempre que era São José.
Os homens punham o chapéu saíam fumando
E eu tinha raiva de ser menino porque não podia ir ver o fogo

Rua da União . . .
Como eram lindos os nomes das ruas da minha infância
Rua do Sol
(Tenho medo que hoje se chame do Dr. Fulano de Tal)
Atrás de casa ficava a Rua da Saudade . . .
. . . onde se ia fumar escondido
Do lado de lá era o cais da Rua da Aurora . . .
. . . onde se ia pescar escondido
Capiberibe
— Capibaribe

Lá longe o sertãozinho de Caxangá
Banheiros de palha

Run rabbit!
Don't run!

In the distance the little girls' petal-soft voices sung out
     in varied tones:

Rosebush, give me a rose
Carnation, give me a bud

(Of those roses many a rose
must have died in the bud . . .)

Suddenly
          in the far corners of the night
                              a bell

One grown-up said:
"Fire in Saint Anthony!"
Another exclaimed, "No, in Saint John!"
Totônio Rodrigues always thought it was Saint John.
The men put on their hats and went out, smoking
and I hated being a boy because I couldn't go with them
     to see the fire

Union Street . . .
The streets of my childhood had such lovely names!
Sun Street
(I hate to think they may have renamed it after some So-and-So)
Behind the house, Nostalgia Street . . .
     . . . where we used to sneak a smoke
On the other side the Dawn Street wharf . . .
     . . . where we used to fish in secret.
Capiberibe
—Capibaribe

There way in the distance, the fields of Caxangá
and its straw bathhouses

Um dia eu vi uma moça nuinha no banho
Fiquei parado o coração batendo
Ela se riu
                    Foi o meu primeiro alumbramento

Cheia! As cheias! Barro boi morto árvores destroços redomoinho
                                                      [sumiu
E nos pegões da ponte do trem de ferro os caboclos destemidos em
                                          [jangadas de bananeiras

Novenas
        Cavalhadas
Eu me deitei no colo da menina e ela começou a passar a mão nos
                                              [meus cabelos
Capiberibe
— Capibaribe

Rua da União onde todas as tardes passava a preta das bananas
                    Com o xale vistoso de pano da Costa
E o vendedor de roletes de cana
O de amendoim
        que se chamava midubim e não era torrado era cozido

Me lembro de todos os pregões:
        Ovos frescos e baratos
        Dez ovos por uma pataca
Foi há muito tempo . . .

A vida não me chegava pelos jornais nem pelos livros
Vinha da boca do povo na língua errada do povo
Língua certa do povo
Porque ele é que fala gostoso o português do Brasil
        Ao passo que nós
                O que fazemos
                É macaquear
                A sintaxe lusíada
A vida com uma porção de coisas que eu não entendia bem
Terras que não sabia onde ficavam

One day I saw a girl completely naked in her bath
I froze there, my heart beating wildly
She laughed
                    It was my first ecstatic vision

Flood! The floods! Mud dead ox trees debris whirlpools
        —all gone
And between the pillars of the railroad bridge daredevil
        country boys in rafts of banana logs

Novenas
            Cavalcades
I lay my head in the girl's lap and she began to run her fingers
        through my hair
Capiberibe
—Capibaribe

Union Street where every afternoon the black woman who sold
        bananas passed by in her bright coarse shawl
and the sugar cane peddler
and the vendor of the peanuts
        we called beenuts and that were boiled instead of roasted

I remember all their chants:
        Eggs, fresh and cheap
        Ten eggs for a quarter
That was so long ago . . .

Life didn't reach me through newspapers or books
but came from the mouth of the people, bad speech of the people
good speech of the people
because it's the people who speak Brazilian Portuguese with gusto
        while we
        all we do
        is imitate, monkey see, monkey do
        the language of the classics
Life with a whole slew of things I didn't really understand
Territories for me yet uncharted

Recife . . .
                Rua da União . . .
                                A casa de meu avô . . .
Nunca pensei que ela acabasse!
Tudo lá parecia impregnado de eternidade

Recife . . .
                Meu avô morto.
Recife morto, Recife bom, Recife brasileiro como a casa de
                                                [meu avô

POEMA TIRADO DE UMA NOTÍCIA DE JORNAL

João Gostoso era carregador de feira-livre e morava no morro da
                        [Babilônia num barracão sem número
Uma noite ele chegou no bar Vinte de Novembro
Bebeu
Cantou
Dançou
Depois se atirou na Lagoa Rodrigo de Freitas e morreu afogado.

TERESA

A primeira vez que vi Teresa
Achei que ela tinha pernas estúpidas
Achei também que a cara parecia uma perna

Quando vi Teresa de novo
Achei que os olhos eram muito mais velhos que o resto do corpo
Os olhos nasceram e ficaram dez anos esperando que o resto do
                                                [corpo nascesse)

Recife . . .
> Union Street
>> My grandfather's home . . .
I never thought that house could disappear!
Everything there seemed charged with eternity

Recife . . .
> My grandfather, dead.
Recife, now dead, bighearted Recife, Recife Brazilian as my
grandfather's home.

FOUND POEM

John Luscious was a carrier-for-hire in the open-air market
and lived in an unnumbered shack on Babylon Hill
One night he went to the Twentieth of November Bar
drank
sang
danced
then threw himself into the Rodrigo de Freitas Lagoon and
drowned.

TERESA

The first time I saw Teresa
I thought she had ridiculous legs.
I also thought her face looked like a leg.

When I saw Teresa a second time
I thought her eyes must be a great deal older than the rest of her.
(Her eyes had been born and waited ten years for the rest of her
body.)

Da terceira vez não vi mais nada
Os céus se misturaram com a terra
E o espírito de Deus voltou a se mover sobre a face das águas.

A VIRGEM MARIA

O oficial do registro civil, o coletor de impostos, o mor-
    domo da Santa Casa e o administrador do cemitério de
        S. João Batista
Cavaram com enxadas
Com pás
Com as unhas
Com os dentes
Cavaram uma cova mais funda que o meu suspiro de renúncia

Depois me botaram lá dentro
E puseram por cima
As Tábuas da Lei

Mas de lá de dentro do fundo da treva do chão da cova
Eu ouvia a vozinha da Virgem Maria
Dizer que fazia sol lá fora
Dizer i n s i s t e n t e m e n t e
Que fazia sol lá fora.

ORAÇÃO NO SACO DE MANGARATIBA

Nossa Senhora me dê paciência
Para estes mares para esta vida!
Me dê paciência pra que eu não caia
Pra que eu não pare nesta existência
Tão mal cumprida tão mais comprida
Do que a restinga de Marambaia! . . .

The third time I no longer saw a thing.
The heavens mingled with the earth
And the spirit of the Lord once again moved over the face of the
    waters.

THE VIRGIN MARY

The keeper of the civil registry, the tax collector, the hospital
    director and the overseer of the St. John the Baptist
    Cemetery
dug with spades
with shovels
with fingernails
and teeth,
dug a grave deeper than my sigh of resignation.

Then they threw me in
and placed on top
the Tables of the Law.

But there deep down, down there so deep within the dark
I heard the Virgin Mary's soft small voice
saying that the sun was shining out there
i n s i s t i n g
that the sun was shining.

PRAYER ON MANGARATIBA BAY

Lady give me patience
for these waters, for this life.
Give me patience not to slip,
not to desist in this existence
so full of longing, so much longer
than the shoals of Marambaia!

O MAJOR

O major morreu.
Reformado.
Veterano da guerra do Paraguai.
Herói da ponte de Itororó.

Não quis honras militares.
Não quis discursos.

Apenas
À hora do enterro
O corneteiro de um batalhão de linha
Deu à boca do túmulo
O toque de silêncio.

CUNHANTÃ

Vinha do Pará
Chamava Siquê.
Quatro anos. Escurinha. O riso gutural da raça.
Piá branca nenhuma corria mais do que ela.

Tinha uma cicatriz no meio da testa:
— Que foi isto, Siquê?
Com voz de detrás da garganta, a boquinha tuíra:
    — Minha mãe (a madrasta) estava costurando
    Disse vai ver se tem fogo
    Eu soprei eu soprei eu soprei não vi fogo
    Aí ela se levantou e esfregou com minha cabeça
    na brasa

Riu, riu, riu . . .

Uêrêquitáua.
O ventilador era a coisa que roda.
Quando se machucava, dizia: Ai Zizus!

THE MAJOR

The major died.
Retired.
Veteran of the Paraguayan War.
Hero of the Bridge of Itororó.

He didn't want military honors.
He didn't want flowery speeches.

His burial was just
this—
an army bugler gave
a salute of Taps
beside his grave.

CUNHANTÃ

She came from Pará.
Name, Siquê.
Four years old. Dark skin. Throaty laugh.
No white urchin could run faster.

A scar in the middle of her forehead.
"What happened here, Siquê?"
A voice from deep within the throat, the small dirty mouth:
    "My mother [her stepmother] was sewing.
    She told me to see to the fire.
    I blew and blew but no fire.
    So she got up and stirred the ashes with my head."

And the child laughed and laughed and laughed . . .

Uêrêquitáua.
The fan was "that thing that turns."
Whenever she hurt herself she said, "Oh Chee-zus!"

ORAÇÃO A TERESINHA DO MENINO JESUS

Perdi o jeito de sofrer.
Ora essa.
Não sinto mais aquele gosto cabotino da tristeza.
Quero alegria! Me dá alegria,
Santa Teresa!
Santa Teresa não, Teresinha . . .
Teresinha . . . Teresinha . . .
Teresinha do Menino Jesus.

Me dá alegria!
Me dá a força de acreditar de novo

No
Pelo Sinal
Da Santa
Cruz!
Me dá alegria! Me dá alegria,
Santa Teresa! . . .
Santa Teresa não, Teresinha . . .
Teresinha do Menino Jesus.

ANDORINHA

Andorinha lá fora está dizendo:
— "Passei o dia à toa, à toa!"

Andorinha, andorinha, minha cantiga é mais triste!
Passei a vida à toa, à toa . . .

PRAYER TO TERESINHA OF LITTLE LORD JESUS

I've lost the hang of suffering.
For sure!
I no longer feel that pretentious taste for sadness.
I want happiness! Give me happiness,
Saint Teresa!
No, not Saint Teresa but Teresinha . . .
Teresinha . . . Teresinha . . .
Teresinha of Little Lord Jesus.

Give me happiness!
Give me the strength to believe anew

in the
Sign of the Cross,
of the Holy
Cross!
Give me happiness! Give me happiness,
Saint Teresa! . . .
Not Saint Teresa but Teresinha . . .
Teresinha of Little Lord Jesus.

SWALLOW

The swallow there outside is saying:
—"I've whiled away my day!"

Swallow, swallow, my song's sadder.
I've whiled my life away. . . .

PROFUNDAMENTE

Quando ontem adormeci
Na noite de São João
Havia alegria e rumor
Estrondos de bombas luzes de Bengala
Vozes cantigas e risos
Ao pé das fogueiras acesas.

No meio da noite despertei
Não ouvi mais vozes nem risos
Apenas balões
Passavam errantes
Silenciosamente
Apenas de vez em quando
O ruído de um bonde
Cortava o silêncio

Como um túnel.
Onde estavam os que há pouco
Dançavam
Cantavam
E riam
Ao pé das fogueiras acesas?

— Estavam todos dormindo
Estavam todos deitados
Dormindo
Profundamente

Quando eu tinha seis anos
Não pude ver o fim da festa de São João
Porque adormeci

Hoje não ouço mais as vozes daquele tempo
Minha avó
Meu avô
Totônio Rodrigues

IN A SOUND SLEEP

When I fell asleep yesterday
—on St. John's Eve—
there was merrymaking, noise
the boom of firecrackers, the blaze of Roman candles
voices, laughter, song
beside the glowing bonfires.

I woke in the middle of the night
and no longer heard voices or laughter.
Only fire balloons
drifted by
silently.
Only from time to time
the noise of a trolley car
cut through the silence

like a tunnel.
Where were those who just a while ago were
dancing
singing
laughing
beside the glowing bonfires?

—They were all sleeping
they were all stretched out
asleep,
in a sound sleep.

When I was six years old
I didn't get to see the end of St. John's Eve
because I fell asleep.

I no longer hear the voices of that time today:
my grandmother
my grandfather
Totônio Rodrigues

Tomásia
Rosa
Onde estão todos eles?
— Estão todos dormindo
Estão todos deitados
Dormindo
Profundamente.

MADRIGAL TÃO ENGRAÇADINHO

Teresa, você é a coisa mais bonita que eu vi até hoje na
    minha vida, inclusive o porquinho-da-índia que me de-
    ram quando eu tinha seis anos.

NOTURNO DA PARADA AMORIM

O violoncelista estava a meio do Concerto de Schumann

Subitamente o coronel ficou transportado e começou a gri-
    tar: — *"Je vois des anges! Je vois des anges!"* — E
    deixou-se escorregar sentado pela escada abaixo.

O telefone tilintou.
Alguém chamava? . . . Alguém pedia socorro? . . .

Mas do outro lado não vinha senão o rumor de um pranto
    desesperado! . . .

(Eram três horas.
Todas as agências postais estavam fechadas.
Dentro da noite a voz do coronel continuava gritando:
    —*"Je vois des anges! Je vois des anges!"*)

Tomásia
Rosa
Where are they all?
—They are all sleeping
they are all stretched out
asleep,
in a sound sleep.

SUCH A FUNNY LITTLE MADRIGAL

Teresa, you're the prettiest thing I've ever seen
    in my whole life including the guinea pig they gave me
    when I was six years old.

NOCTURNE OF AMORIM STATION

The cellist was in the middle of the Schumann concert.

Suddenly the colonel went into a trance and started shouting—
    "Je vois des anges! Je vois des anges!"—And he let himself
    go sliding down the bannister.

The telephone jingled.
Was someone calling? . . . Someone asking for help? . . .

But on the other end there was only a desperate sobbing! . . .

(Three o'clock.
All the post offices were closed.
From deep within the night the colonel's voice continued
    to shout: "Je vois des anges! Je vois des anges!")

NA BOCA

Sempre tristíssimas estas cantigas de carnaval
Paixão
Ciúme
Dor daquilo que não se pode dizer

Felizmente existe o álcool na vida
E nos três dias de carnaval éter de lança-perfume
Quem me dera ser como o rapaz desvairado!
O ano passado ele parava diante das mulheres bonitas
E gritava pedindo o esguicho de cloretilo:
— Na boca! Na boca!
Umas davam-lhe as costas com repugnância
Outras porém faziam-lhe a vontade.

Ainda existem mulheres bastante puras para fazer vontade aos
                                                        [viciados

Dorinha meu amor . . .

Se ela fosse bastante pura eu iria agora gritar-lhe como o outro:
— Na boca! Na boca!

MACUMBA DE PAI ZUSÉ

Na macumba do Encantado
Nego véio pai de santo fez mandinga
No palacete de Botafogo
Sangue de branca virou água
Foram vê estava morta!

IN THE MOUTH

Always so sad these Carnival songs . . .
passion
jealousy
the pain of what can't be said.

Fortunately, there is always the bottle
and during the three days of Carnival the perfumed ether
    merrymakers squirt at one another.
How I'd like to be that crackpot boy . . .
Last year he came up to the pretty women
shouting that he wanted a shot of ether
—"In the mouth! In the mouth!"
Some of them turned their backs
but others gave him what he wanted.

There are still women pure enough to want to please an addict.

Dorinha, my love . . .

If she were pure enough I'd shout at her just like that boy:
"In the mouth! In the mouth!"

VOODOO AT PAI ZUSÉ'S

At the voodoo in the Spellbound district
the old black priest worked his magic—
In the Botafogo mansion
the white woman's blood turned to water.
They went to see and she was dead!

NOTURNO DA RUA DA LAPA

A janela estava aberta. Para o quê, não sei, mas o que entrava era o vento dos lupanares, de mistura com o eco que se partia nas curvas cicloidais, e fragmentos do hino da bandeira.

Não posso atinar no que eu fazia: se meditava, se morria de espanto ou se vinha de muito longe.

Nesse momento (oh! por que precisamente nesse momento? . . .) é que penetrou no quarto o bicho que voava, o articulado implacável, implacável!

Compreendi desde logo não haver possibilidade nenhuma de evasão. Nascer de novo também não adiantava. — A bomba de flit! pensei comigo, é um inseto!

Quando o jacto fumigatório partiu, nada mudou em mim; os sinos da redenção continuaram em silêncio; nenhuma porta se abriu nem fechou. Mas o monstruoso animal FICOU MAIOR. Senti que ele não morreria nunca mais, nem sairia, conquanto não houvesse no aposento nenhum busto de Palas, nem na minh'alma, o que é pior, a recordação persistente de alguma extinta Lenora.

CABEDELO

Viagem à roda do mundo
Numa casquinha de noz:
Estive em Cabedelo.
O macaco me ofereceu cocos.

Ó maninha, ó maninha,
Tu não estavas comigo! . . .

— Estavas? . . .

LAPA STREET NOCTURNE

The window was open. Why, I couldn't say, but it let in the
breeze from the brothels mingled with the echo emanating in
cycloid curves together with fragments of the national anthem.

I can't imagine what I might have been doing at the time—
meditating, dying of fright, or just arriving from a distance.

It was in this moment (oh why precisely this moment?) that a
winged creature invaded my room, a relentless, absolutely
relentless specimen.

I immediately saw escape would be impossible. To be born
again would do no good.—"The insect repellent! Quick!"
I thought to myself, "It is an insect!"

The lethal jet had no effect; I felt no different; the bells
of redemption remained silent; no door opened or closed. But the
monstrous creature GOT BIGGER. I thought it would never die or
disappear, although there was no bust of Pallas in the bedroom.
Nor was there—what is worse—within my soul the persistent
memory of any long-departed Lenore.

CABEDELO

Journey around the world
in a little nutshell.
I was in Cabedelo.
The monkey offered me coconuts.

Oh sister, little sister,
you weren't with me! . . .

Were you? . . .

IRENE NO CÉU

Irene preta
Irene boa
Irene sempre de bom humor.

Imagino Irene entrando no céu:
— Licença, meu branco!
E São Pedro bonachão:
— Entra, Irene. Você não precisa pedir licença.

NAMORADOS

O rapaz chegou-se para junto da moça e disse:
— Antônia, ainda não me acostumei com o seu corpo, com
a sua cara.

A moça olhou de lado e esperou.

— Você não sabe quando a gente é criança e de repente vê
uma lagarta listada?

A moça se lembrava:
— A gente fica olhando . . .

A meninice brincou de novo nos olhos dela.

O rapaz prosseguiu com muita doçura:

— Antônia, você parece uma lagarta listada.

A moça arregalou os olhos, fez exclamações.

O rapaz concluiu:
— Antônia, você é engraçada! Você parece louca.

IRENE IN HEAVEN

Black Irene
Kind Irene
Irene always in a good mood.

I imagine Irene entering heaven:
—"Say there, sir, is it all right if I come in?"
And Saint Peter, good-natured,
—"Come on in, Irene. You don't have to stand there asking."

BOY AND GIRL

The boy went over to his girl and said,
—"Antônia, I still haven't gotten used to your face, your body."

The girl looked away and waited.

"You know how it is when you're a kid and suddenly see
    a striped caterpillar?"

The girl recalled,
    "We'd stare . . . "

Her childhood danced once more within her eyes.

The boy went on very tenderly:

    "Antônia, you look like a striped caterpillar."

The girl opened her eyes wide, protested.

The boy concluded:
—"Antônia, you're funny! You're really crazy."

VOU-ME EMBORA PRA PASÁRGADA

Vou-me embora pra Pasárgada
Lá sou amigo do rei
Lá tenho a mulher que eu quero
Na cama que escolherei
Vou-me embora pra Pasárgada

Vou-me embora pra Pasárgada
Aqui eu não sou feliz
Lá a existência é uma aventura
De tal modo inconseqüente
Que Joana a Louca de Espanha
Rainha e falsa demente
Vem a ser contraparente
Da nora que nunca tive

E como farei ginástica
Andarei de bicicleta
Montarei em burro brabo
Subirei no pau-de-sebo
Tomarei banhos de mar!
E quando estiver cansado
Deito na beira do rio
Mando chamar a mãe-d'água
Pra me contar as histórias
Que no tempo de eu menino
Rosa vinha me contar
Vou-me embora pra Pasárgada

Em Pasárgada tem tudo
É outra civilização
Tem um processo seguro
De impedir a concepção
Tem telefone automático
Tem alcalóide à vontade
Tem prostitutas bonitas
Para a gente namorar

PASÁRGADA

I'm heading off to Pasárgada
—there I'm a friend of the king,
there I can have any woman
anytime, any bed, anything!
I'm heading off to Pasárgada.

I'm heading off to Pasárgada.
Here I can't get what I need.
There, you see, life's an adventure
so unpredictably free
that Mad Joan of Spain's a relation
of the daughter-in-law never-to-be.

And all the sports that I'll play there . . .
I'll go bicycling (bicycling, me!),
ride a wild burro,
climb a greased pole,
and swim for miles in the sea.
And then when I'm tired I'll stretch out
beside the river to dream.
To hear those old tales Rosa told once
I'll summon the Mother-of-Streams.
I'm heading off to Pasárgada!

Pasárgada has all you could want.
(Another civilization, I'm told.)
They've got birth control,
they've got dope there,
they've got dial telephones.
They are plenty of good-looking hookers
just waiting for someone to hold.

E quando eu estiver mais triste
Mas triste de não ter jeito
Quando de noite me der
Vontade de me matar
— Lá sou amigo do rei —
Terei a mulher que eu quero
Na cama que escolherei
Vou-me embora pra Pasárgada.

O IMPOSSÍVEL CARINHO

Escuta, eu não quero contar-te o meu desejo
Quero apenas contar-te a minha ternura
Ah se em troca de tanta felicidade que me dás
Eu te pudesse repor
— Eu soubesse repor —
No coração despedaçado
As mais puras alegrias de tua infância!

O ÚLTIMO POEMA

Assim eu quereria o meu último poema

Que fosse terno dizendo as coisas mais simples e menos inten-
[cionais
Que fosse ardente como um soluço sem lágrimas
Que tivesse a beleza das flores quase sem perfume
A pureza da chama em que se consomem os diamantes mais
[límpidos
A paixão dos suicidas que se matam sem explicação.

And when I become even sadder
so sad nothing does any good
when at night all I want
is to die, is to take my own life
—There I'm a friend of the king—
there I can have any woman
anytime, any bed, anything!
I'm heading off to Pasárgada.

IMPOSSIBLE AFFECTION

Listen, I don't want to speak of my desire.
I just want to tell you of my tender feelings.
Ah, if in return for all you give me
I could restore
—if I could only restore—
to your shattered heart
the sheer joy of your childhood!

THE LAST POEM

This is the way I would like my last poem—

tender, saying the simplest and least premeditated things,

ardent, like a sob without tears,
with the beauty of barely fragrant flowers,
the purity of the flame in which the most limpid diamonds
    are consumed,
the passion of suicides who kill themselves without explanation.

ESTRELA DA MANHÃ
MORNING STAR
1936

ESTRELA DA MANHÃ

Eu quero a estrela da manhã
Onde está a estrela da manhã?
Meus amigos meus inimigos
Procurem a estrela da manhã

Ela desapareceu ia nua
Desapareceu com quem?
Procurem por toda parte

Digam que sou um homem sem orgulho
Um homem que aceita tudo
Que me importa?
Eu quero a estrela da manhã

Três dias e três noites
Fui assassino e suicida
Ladrão, pulha, falsário

Virgem mal-sexuada
Atribuladora dos aflitos
Girafa de duas cabeças
Pecai por todos pecai com todos

Pecai com os malandros
Pecai com os sargentos
Pecai com os fuzileiros navais
Pecai de todas as maneiras
Com os gregos e com os troianos
Com o padre e com o sacristão
Com o leproso de Pouso Alto

Depois comigo

MORNING STAR

I want the morning star.
Where could she be?
My friends, my enemies,
search out the morning star.

She left naked.
With whom did she leave?
Search everywhere for her.

Let them call me a man without pride,
a man who will swallow anything.
What's it to me?
I want the morning star.

For three days and three nights
I was a murderer, a suicide,
a thief, a good-for-nothing, a forger.

Unhappily sexed Virgin,
afflictor of the afflicted,
two-headed giraffe,
sin for all, sin with all.

Sin with the no-goods,
sin with the sergeants,
sin with the leathernecks,
sin every way you can
—with the Greeks, with the Trojans,
with the priest, the sacristan,
with the leper from Lofty Perch.

Then come sin with me

Te esperarei com mafuás novenas cavalhadas
                    [comerei terra e direi coisas
                    [de uma ternura tão simples
Que tu desfalecerás

Procurem por toda parte
Pura ou degradada até a última baixeza
Eu quero a estrela da manhã.

CANÇÃO DAS DUAS ÍNDIAS

Entre estas Índias de leste
E as Índias ocidentais
Meu Deus que distância enorme
Quantos Oceanos Pacíficos
Quantos bancos de corais
Quantas frias latitudes!
Ilhas que a tormenta arrasa
Que os terremotos subvertem
Desoladas Marambaias
Sirtes sereias Medéias
Púbis a não poder mais
Altos como a estrela-d'alva
Longínquos como Oceanias
— Brancas, sobrenaturais —
Oh inaccessíveis praias! . . .

POEMA DO BECO

Que importa a paisagem, a Glória, a baía, a linha do horizonte?
— O que eu vejo é o beco.

I'll be waiting for you with amusement parks, novenas, cavalcades
 I'll eat dirt and say things of a tenderness so frank
you'll swoon.

Search everywhere
pure or sunken low as low can go
I want the morning star.

SONG OF THE TWO INDIES

Between these East
and these West Indies,
my God, what an immense expanse
How many Pacific Oceans
how many coral reefs
how many icy latitudes!
Islands the storm levels
and the earthquakes raze
desolate Marambaias
quicksand sirens Medeas
pubis to the nth degree
high like the morning star
distant like the Oceanias
—white, supernatural—
oh inaccessible beaches! . . .

POEM OF THE ALLEY

What does it matter—view, bay, Glória district, skyline?
—What I see is the alley.

BALADA DAS TRÊS MULHERES DO SABONETE ARAXÁ

As três mulheres do sabonete Araxá me invocam, me bouleversam,
[me hipnotizam.
Oh, as três mulheres do sabonete Araxá às 4 horas da tarde!

O meu reino pelas três mulheres do sabonete Araxá!

Que outros, não eu, a pedra cortem
Para brutais vos adorarem,
Ó brancaranas azedas,
Mulatas cor da lua vem saindo cor de prata
Ou celestes africanas:
Que eu vivo, padeço e morro só pelas três mulheres do sabonete
[Araxá!
São amigas, são irmãs, são amantes as três mulheres do sabonete
[Araxá?
São prostitutas, são declamadoras, são acrobatas?
São as três Marias?

Meu Deus, serão as três Marias?

A mais nua é doirada borboleta.
Se a segunda casasse, eu ficava safado da vida,
[dava pra beber e nunca mais telefonava.
Mas se a terceira morresse . . . Oh, então, nunca mais a minha
[vida outrora teria
[sido um festim!
Se me perguntassem: Queres ser estrela? queres ser rei? queres
[uma ilha no Pacífico?
[um bangalô em Copacabana?
Eu responderia: Não quero nada disso, tetrarca. Eu só quero as
[três mulheres do sabonete Araxá:

O meu reino pelas três mulheres do sabonete Araxá!

BALLAD OF THE THREE WOMEN ON THE ARAXÁ SOAP WRAPPER

The three women on the Araxá soap wrapper call out to me,
    bowl me over, mesmerize me.
Oh the three women on the Araxá soap wrapper at four o'clock
    in the afternoon!
My kingdom for the three women on the Araxá soap wrapper!

Let others, not me, cut through stone
to worship you, oh heartless ones,
oh bitter brancaranas
silvery, moon-colored mulattas
or celestial africanas
Me, I live, I pine, I die for the three women on the Araxá
    soap wrapper and them alone!
Are they friends, sisters, lovers, the three women
    on the Araxá soap wrapper?
Are they whores, orators, acrobats?
Are they the three Marys?

Good Lord, could they be the three Marys?

The most naked of the three is a golden butterfly.
If the second were to marry, I'd be thoroughly pissed off,
    take to the bottle and give up talking on the phone.
But if the third one died—Oh then my life would never again
    be a celebration!

If they should ask me, "Would you like to be a star? A king?
    Would you like a Pacific isle? A bungalow in Copacabana?"

I'd say, "Nothing of the sort, my lord. All I want
    is the three women on the Araxá soap wrapper:

My kingdom for the three women on the Araxá soap wrapper!

A FILHA DO REI

Aquela cor de cabelos
Que eu vi na filha do rei
— Mas vi tão subitamente —
Será a mesma cor da axila,
Do maravilhoso pente?
Como agora o saberei?
Vi-a tão subitamente!
Ela passou como um raio:

Só vi a cor dos cabelos.
Mas o corpo, a luz do corpo? . . .
Como seria o seu corpo? . . .
Jamais o conhecerei!

CANTIGA

Nas ondas da praia
Nas ondas do mar
Quero ser feliz
Quero me afogar.

Nas ondas da praia
Quem vem me beijar?
Quero a estrela-d'alva
Rainha do mar.

Quero ser feliz
Nas ondas do mar
Quero esquecer tudo
Quero descansar.

THE KING'S DAUGHTER

Could the hair
of the king's daughter—(Oh
I got such a fleeting look)
—could her hair be the same color
as her underarms,
her marvelous sex?
And how will I ever know?
(I got such a fleeting look!)
She breezed by like a sunbeam
(her hair is all I saw).
But her body, her body's glow?
What color might be her body?
That body I will never know!

POEM SET TO MUSIC

In the waves of the beach
the waves of the sea,
I want to be happy,
to drown in the deep.

In the waves of the beach,
who will kiss me?
I want the dawn star,
queen of the sea.

I want to be happy
in the waves of the sea,
I want to forget,
to find rest, to be free.

ORAÇÃO A NOSSA SENHORA DA BOA MORTE

Fiz tantos versos a Teresinha . . .
Versos tão tristes, nunca se viu!
Pedi-lhe coisas. O que eu pedia
Era tão pouco! Não era glória . . .
Nem era amores . . . Nem foi dinheiro . . .
Pedia apenas mais alegria:
Santa Teresa nunca me ouviu!

Para outras santas voltei os olhos.
Porém as santas são impassíveis
Como as mulheres que me enganaram.
Desenganei-me das outras santas
(Pedi a muitas, rezei a tantas)
Até que um dia me apresentaram
A Santa Rita dos Impossíveis.

Fui despachado de mãos vazias!
Dei volta ao mundo, tentei a sorte.
Nem alegrias mais peço agora,
Que eu sei o avesso das alegrias.
Tudo que viesse, viria tarde!
O que na vida procurei sempre,
— Meus impossíveis de Santa Rita —
Dar-me-eis um dia, não é verdade?
Nossa Senhora da Boa Morte!

MOMENTO NUM CAFÉ

Quando o enterro passou
Os homens que se achavam no café
Tiraram o chapéu maquinalmente
Saudavam o morto distraídos
Estavam todos voltados para a vida
Absortos na vida
Confiantes da vida.

PRAYER TO OUR LADY OF THE PAINLESS DEATH

I wrote so many verses for my little Teresa . . .
Sadder verses don't exist!
I asked her for things. I asked
so little! Not glory . . .
not love . . . not money . . .
—Just a bit more happiness:
Saint Teresa never heard my prayers!

I turned my eyes toward other saints
but they proved indifferent
like the women who deceived me.
I lost faith in them
(I had beseeched so many, prayed so much)
until one day they introduced me
to Saint Rita of the Impossible Desires.

I was packed off empty-handed!
I circled the globe, trying my luck.
Now I don't even ask for happiness
because I know its underside.
All that I'd ever wanted would come too late!
—My impossible desire for my Saint Rita!
You'll reward my patience one day, won't you?
Our Lady of the Painless Death!

MOMENT IN A CAFÉ

When the funeral procession went by
the men who happened to be in the café
mechanically took off their hats,
absentmindedly acknowledging the dead man.
They were caught up in life,
absorbed in life,
confident of life.

Um no entanto se descobriu num gesto largo e demorado
Olhando o esquife longamente
Este sabia que a vida é uma agitação feroz e sem finalidade
Que a vida é traição
E saudava a matéria que passava
Liberta para sempre da alma extinta.

CONTRIÇÃO

Quero banhar-me nas águas límpidas
Quero banhar-me nas águas puras
Sou a mais baixa das criaturas
      Me sinto sórdido

Confiei às feras as minhas lágrimas
Rolei de borco pelas calçadas
Cobri meu rosto de bofetadas
      Meu Deus valei-me

Vozes da infância contai a história
Da vida boa que nunca veio
E eu caia ouvindo-a no calmo seio
      Da eternidade.

SACHA E O POETA

Quando o poeta aparece,
Sacha levanta os olhos claros,
Onde a surpresa é o sol que vai nascer.

O poeta a seguir diz coisas incríveis,
Desce ao fogo central da Terra,
Sobe na ponta mais alta das nuvens,

One, however, took off his hat in a slow, expansive gesture,
watching the coffin a long time.
This man knew that life is a fierce and senseless agitation,
that life is betrayal . . .
and he saluted the body that passed
free forever of the snuffed-out soul.

CONTRITION

I want to bathe in the bright waters
I want to bathe in the clear waters
I am the lowest of the low
        I feel vile.

I entrusted my tears to the wild beasts
I tumbled head over heels down the sidewalk
I slapped my own face over and over
        Oh God, help me!

Voices of childhood, tell the story
of the happily-ever-after that never was
and hearing it, let me fall into the calm bosom
        of eternity.

SACHA AND THE POET

When the poet appears,
Sacha raises clear eyes
in which surprise is the sun about to dawn.

The poet goes on to say amazing things.
He descends to the earth's fiery core,
he rises on the peak of clouds.

Faz gurugutu pif paf,
Dança de velho,
Vira Exu.
Sacha sorri como o primeiro arco-íris.

O poeta estende os braços, Sacha vem com ele.

A serenidade voltou de muito longe.
Que se passou do outro lado?
Sacha mediunizada
— Ah—pa—papapá—papá —
Transmite em Morse ao poeta
A última mensagem dos Anjos.

JACQUELINE

Jacqueline morreu menina.
Jacqueline morta era mais bonita do que os anjos.
Os anjos! . . . Bem sei que não os há em parte alguma.
Há é mulheres extraordinariamente belas que morrem ainda
                                                    [meninas.

Houve tempo em que olhei para os teus retratos de menina
                              [como olho agora para a pequena
                              [imagem de Jacqueline morta.
Eras tão bonita!
Eras tão bonita, que merecerias ter morrido na idade de
                                                    [Jacqueline

— Pura como Jacqueline.

He says "gurugutu pif paf,"
he dances like an old man,
he becomes the trickster god, Exu.
Sacha smiles like the first rainbow.

The poet extends his arms, Sacha accompanies him.

Calm has descended once more from afar.
What happened on the other side?
Sacha in a trance says—
—Ah—pa—papapá—papá—
transmitting to the poet in Morse code
the latest message of the angels.

JACQUELINE

Jacqueline died while still a little girl.
In death, Jacqueline was prettier than the angels.
The angels! . . . I know very well they don't exist.
There are only extraordinarily beautiful women who die as girls.

There was a time when I looked on pictures of you as a girl
        as I now look on the portrait of the dead Jacqueline.

You were so pretty!
You were so pretty you deserved to have died at the same age
        as Jacqueline.

—Pure as Jacqueline.

D. JANAÍNA

D. Janaína
Sereia do mar
D. Janaína
De maiô encarnado
D. Janaína
Vai se banhar.

D. Janaína
Princesa do mar
D. Janaína
Tem muitos amores
É o rei do Congo
É o rei de Aloanda
É o sultão-dos-matos
É S. Salavá!

Saravá saravá
D. Janaína
Rainha do mar

D. Janaína
Princesa do mar
Dai-me licença
Pra eu também brincar
No vosso reinado

TRUCIDARAM O RIO

Prendei o rio
Maltratai o rio
Trucidai o rio

DONA JANAÍNA

Dona Janaína,
siren of the sea,
Dona Janaína
pretty as can be
in her bright red swimsuit
goes swimming in the deep.

Dona Janaína,
princess of the sea,
Janaína with her suitors
far as the eye can see—
There's the king of Congo,
the sultan-of-the-dell,
the king of Aloanda,
Saint Salavá as well.

All hail, Janaína
Janaína, hail to thee
Dona Janaína,
queen of the high sea.

Dona Janaína,
princess of the sea,
give me your permission,
please say you'll let me
play, let me play too
in your kingdom.

THEY MURDERED THE RIVER

Dam up the river,
abuse it,
take its life—

A água não morre
A água que é feita
De gotas inermes
Que um dia serão
Maiores que o rio
Grandes como o oceano
Fortes como os gelos
Os gelos polares
Que tudo arrebentam.

TREM DE FERRO

Café com pão
Café com pão
Café com pão

Virge Maria que foi isto maquinista?

Agora sim
Café com pão
Agora sim
Voa, fumaça
Corre, cerca
Ai seu foguista
Bota fogo
Na fornalha
Que eu preciso
Muita força
Muita força
Muita força

Oô . . .
Foge, bicho
Foge, povo
Passa ponte
Passa poste

The water doesn't die,
the water is composed
of defenseless droplets
that one day will be
greater than any river,
vast as the ocean,
strong as ice,
the polar ice
that shatters all before it.

IRON HORSE

Bread-'n-coffee
bread-'n-coffee
bread-'n-coffee

Holy moly, what was that, engineer?

That's more like it
bread-'n-coffee
That's more like it
Fly, smoke
Run by, railing
Hey there, Mr. Stoker,
stoke up the fire
in the furnace
'cause I need
lots of force
lots of force
lots of force.

Whoo-whoo . . .
Out of my way, four-legs,
Out of my way, folks
The bridge goes by,
the light post goes by,

Passa pasto
Passa boi
Passa boiada
Passa galho
De ingazeira
Debruçada
No riacho
Que vontade
De cantar!

Oô . . .
Quando me prendero
No canaviá
Cada pé de cana
Era um oficiá
Oô . . .
Menina bonita
Do vestido verde
Me dá tua boca
Pra matá minha sede
Oô . . .
Vou mimbora vou mimbora
Não gosto daqui
Nasci no sertão
Sou de Ouricuri
Oô . . .

Vou depressa
Vou correndo
Vou na toda
Que só levo
Pouca gente
Pouca gente
Pouca gente . . .

the fields go by
the ox goes by,
the oxen
and the branch
of the mimosa tree curved over
the little stream
How you make me want to sing!

Whoo-whoo . . .
When they cum and got me
thar amidst the cane,
every stalk of sugar
had a shuriff's name.
Whoo-whoo . . .
Girl, purty girl
in your green dress,
come kiss my mouth,
slake my thirst with a "yes."
Whoo-whoo . . .
I'm leavin', I'm leavin'
this ain't fur me
cuz I'm from the backlands
of Oreekooreé.
Whoo-whoo . . .

I rush by
I run by
at full speed
since I carry
few riders
few riders
few riders.

TRAGÉDIA BRASILEIRA

Misael, funcionário da Fazenda, com 63 anos de idade,
    Conheceu Maria Elvira na Lapa — prostituída, com sí-
filis, dermite nos dedos, uma aliança empenhada e os dentes
em petição de miséria.
    Misael tirou Maria Elvira da vida, instalou-a num so-
brado no Estácio, pagou médico, dentista, manicura . . . Dava
tudo quanto ela queria.

    Quando Maria Elvira se apanhou de boca bonita, arran-
jou logo um namorado.
    Misael não queria escândalo. Podia dar uma surra, um
tiro, uma facada. Não fez nada disso: mudou de casa.

    Viveram três anos assim.
    Toda vez que Maria Elvira arranjava namorado, Mi-
sael mudava de casa.
    Os amantes moraram no Estácio, Rocha, Catete, Rua
General Pedra, Olaria, Ramos, Bom Sucesso, Vila Isabel,
Rua Marquês de Sapucaí, Niterói, Encantado, Rua Clapp,
outra vez no Estácio, Todos os Santos, Catumbi, Lavradio,
Boca do Mato, Inválidos . . .
    Por fim na Rua da Constituição, onde Misael, privado de
sentidos e de inteligência, matou-a com seis tiros, e a polí-
cia foi encontrá-la caída em decúbito dorsal, vestida de
organdi azul.

CONTO CRUEL

A uremia não o deixava dormir. A filha deu uma injeção
de sedol.
    — Papai verá que vai dormir.

BRAZILIAN TRAGEDY

Misael, employee of the Treasury Department, age sixty-three, got to know Maria Elvira in the Grotto—a whore with syphilis, a rash on her fingers, a wedding ring in hock and teeth rotten to the point of no return.

Misael rescued Maria Elvira from the Life, set her up in a nice house in Junction City, paid for the doctor, the dentist, the manicurist. He gave her everything her heart desired.

When Maria Elvira found herself with a pretty mouth she ran out and got a boyfriend.

Misael didn't want trouble. He could have given her a beating, a bullet through the head, a knife in the belly. But he didn't; he just found them another place to live.

They went on like this for three years.

Every time Maria Elvira took up with a new man, Misael found another house.

The lovers lived in Junction City, Boulder, The Sties, General Stone Street, Brickyard, Branches, Lucky Strike, Villa Isabel, Marquis of Sapucaí Street, Spellbound, Clapp Street, again in Junction City, All Saints, Take-Your-Chance, Tillage, Edgewood, Soldiers' Rest . . .

And finally in Constitution Street where Misael, at his wits' end, shot her six times and the police found her decumbent and decked out in blue organdy.

CRUEL TALE

His uremia wouldn't let him sleep. The daughter injected a sedative.

"Now you'll see how well you sleep, Dad . . . "

O pai aquietou-se e esperou. Dez minutos . . . Quinze
minutos . . . Vinte minutos . . . Quem disse que o sono che-
gava? Então, ele implorou chorando:
— Meu Jesus Cristinho!
Mas Jesus Cristinho nem se incomodou.

RONDÓ DOS CAVALINHOS

Os cavalinhos correndo,
E nós, cavalões, comendo . . .
Tua beleza, Esmeralda,
Acabou me enlouquecendo.

Os cavalinhos correndo,
E nós, cavalões, comendo . . .
O sol tão claro lá fora,
E em minh'alma — anoitecendo!

Os cavalinhos correndo,
E nós cavalões, comendo . . .
Alfonso Reyes partindo,
E tanta gente ficando . . .

Os cavalinhos correndo,
E nós, cavalões, comendo . . .
A Itália falando grosso,
A Europa se avacalhando . . .

Os cavalinhos correndo,
E nós cavalões, comendo . . .
O Brasil politicando,
Nossa! A poesia morrendo . . .
O sol tão claro lá fora,
O sol tão claro, Esmeralda,
E em minh'alma — anoitecendo!

The father forced himself to relax and waited. Ten
minutes . . . Fifteen . . . Twenty . . . Who said he was going to
sleep? Finally he pleaded in a sob:
"My Sweet Jesus!"
But Sweet Jesus didn't take the slightest notice.

RONDEAU OF THE LITTLE HORSES

The little horses fleeing
and we, big horses, eating . . .
Your beauty, Esmeralda,
finally drove me wild.

The little horses fleeing
and we, big horses, eating . . .
The sun so bright outside,
and in my soul—night coming on!

The little horses fleeing
and, we big horses, eating
Alfonso Reyes departing
and so many people sitting tight . . .

The little horses fleeing
and we, big horses, eating . . .
Italy talking big
and Europe cowering . . .

The little horses fleeing
and we, big horses, eating . . .
Brazil talk-talk-talking
—Lord!—while poetry dies on the vine . . .
The sun so bright outside,
The sun so bright, Esmeralda,
and in my soul—night coming on!

A ESTRELA E O ANJO

Vésper caiu cheia de pudor na minha cama
Vésper em cuja ardência não havia a menor parcela de sen-
                                        [sualidade
Enquanto eu gritava o seu nome três vezes
Dois grandes botões de rosa murcharam

E o meu anjo da guarda quedou-se de mãos postas no desejo
                              [insatisfeito de Deus.

STAR AND ANGEL

The evening star fell, full of shame, into my bed.
The evening star in whose blaze there was not the least erotic
impulse.

During the time it took to shout her name three times
two enormous rosebuds shriveled up and died

And my guardian angel remained, hands joined,
in the unrequited desire of the Lord.

LIRA DOS CINQÜENT'ANOS
LYRE OF FIFTY YEARS
1940

POEMA DESENTRANHADO DE UMA PROSA DE AUGUSTO FREDERICO SCHMIDT

A luz da tua poesia é triste mas pura.
A solidão é o grande sinal do teu destino.
O pitoresco, as cores vivas, o mistério e calor dos outros seres te
                                    [interessam realmente
Mas tu estás apartado de tudo isso, porque vives na companhia
                                    [dos teus desaparecidos,
Dos que brincaram e cantaram um dia à luz das fogueiras
                                    [de S. João
E hoje estão para sempre dormindo profundamente.
Da poesia feita como quem ama e quem morre
Caminhaste para uma poesia de quem vive e recebe a tristeza
Naturalmente
—Como o céu escuro recebe a companhia das primeiras estrelas.

O MARTELO

As rodas rangem na curva dos trilhos
Inexoravelmente.
Mas eu salvei do meu naufrágio
Os elementos mais cotidianos.
O meu quarto resume o passado em todas as casas que habitei.

Dentro da noite
No cerne duro da cidade
Me sinto protegido.
Do jardim do convento
Vem o pio da coruja.
Doce como um arrulho de pomba.
Sei que amanhã quando acordar
Ouvirei o martelo do ferreiro
Bater corajoso o seu cântico de certezas.

POEM DISENTANGLED FROM A PROSE PIECE
BY AUGUSTO FREDERICO SCHMIDT

The light of your poetry is sad but clear.
Solitude is what marks your life.
The uniqueness, color, mystery and warmth in others genuinely
        interests you
But you remain aloof because you live amidst your dead

—those who once made merry and sang by the light
            of the St. John's bonfires
and who are now wrapped in a deep and lasting sleep.
You progressed from the poetry of a man who loves and dies
to that of a man who lives, accepting sorrow
with all simplicity
—like the dark sky accepts the company of the first stars.

THE HAMMER

The wheels grind in the curve of the track
inexorably.
But I have shored up from my shipwreck
the most elemental things.
My room resumes the past in all the houses in which I ever lived.

Within the night,
within the hard kernel of the city,
I feel secure.
From the convent garden
comes the owl's hoot.
Melodious as the cooing of a dove.
I know that when I awake tomorrow
I will hear the blacksmith's hammer
bravely beating out its canticle of certainties.

MAÇÃ

Por um lado te vejo como um seio murcho
Pelo outro como um ventre de cujo umbigo pende ainda o cordão
[placentário

És vermelha como o amor divino

Dentro de ti em pequenas pevides
Palpita a vida prodigiosa
Infinitamente

E quedas tão simples
Ao lado de um talher
Num quarto pobre de hotel.

DESAFIO

Não sou barqueiro de vela,
Mas sou um bom remador:
No lago de São Lourenço
Dei prova do meu valor!
Remando contra a corrente,
Ligeiro como a favor,
Contra a neblina enganosa,
Contra o vento zumbidor!
Sou nortista destemido,
Não gaúcho roncador:
No lago de São Lourenço
Dei prova do meu valor!
Uma só coisa faltava
No meu barco remador:
Ver assentado na popa
O vulto do meu amor . . .
Mas isso era bom demais
— Sorriso claro dos anjos,
Graça de Nosso Senhor!

APPLE

On the one hand, I see you as a withered breast.
On the other, as a navel from which the birth cord still dangles.

You are crimson like divine love.

Within you in tiny seeds
prodigious life throbs
without limit.

Yet you remain so simple
beside a fork and knife
in a poor hotel room.

CHALLENGE

I'm not much with a sail
but a good oarsman, I am.
Out there on Lake Saint Lawrence
I proved I am a man.
Paddling against the current
swift, with the greatest of ease
against the treacherous mist
against the whistling breeze.
I'm a fearless son of the north,
not a bragging southern cowhand:
Out there on Lake Saint Lawrence
I proved I am a man.
Only one thing was missing
in my boat, and that was to see
seated in the stern my love's body . . .
but this was too good to be.
—Radiant smile of the angels,
the Lord's favor shining on me.

VERSOS DE NATAL

Espelho, amigo verdadeiro,
Tu refletes as minhas rugas,
Os meus cabelos brancos,
Os meus olhos míopes e cansados.
Espelho, amigo verdadeiro,
Mestre do realismo exato e minucioso,
Obrigado, obrigado!

Mas se fosses mágico,
Penetrarias até ao fundo desse homem triste,
Descobririas o menino que sustenta esse homem,
O menino que não quer morrer,
Que não morrerá senão comigo,
O menino que todos os anos na véspera do Natal
Pensa ainda em pôr os seus chinelinhos atrás da porta.

POUSA A MÃO NA MINHA TESTA

Não te doas do meu silêncio:
Estou cansado de todas as palavras.
Não sabes que te amo?
Pousa a mão na minha testa:
Captarás numa palpitação inefável
O sentido da única palavra essencial
— Amor.

ÁGUA-FORTE

O preto no branco,
O pente na pele:
Pássaro espalmado
No céu quase branco.

CHRISTMAS POEM

Mirror, true friend,
you reflect my wrinkles,
my white hair,
my tired, nearsighted eyes.
Mirror, true friend,
master of exact and scrupulous realism,
thank you, thank you.

But if you were magic,
you would plumb the depths of this sad man,
you would discover the child who sustains this man,
the child who refuses to die,
who won't die except with me,
the child who every Christmas Eve
would still like to leave his slippers behind the door.

REST YOUR HAND ON MY FOREHEAD

Don't let my silence wound you.
I'm just tired of words.
Don't you know I love you?
Put your hand on my forehead:
You will capture in an ineffable pulse
the meaning of the only word that counts
—Love.

AQUA FORTIS

Black on white,
the sex against the skin:
bird cupped within
a sky, near-white.

Em meio do pente,
A concha bivalve
Num mar de escarlata.
Concha, rosa ou tâmara?

No escuro recesso,
As fontes da vida
A sangrar inúteis
Por duas feridas.

Tudo bem oculto
Sob as aparências
Da água-forte simples:
De face, de flanco,
O preto no branco.

A MORTE ABSOLUTA

Morrer.
Morrer de corpo e de alma.
Completamente.

Morrer sem deixar o triste despojo da carne,
A exangue máscara de cera,
Cercada de flores,
Que apodrecerão — felizes! — num dia,
Banhada de lágrimas
Nascidas menos da saudade do que do espanto da morte.

Morrer sem deixar porventura uma alma errante . . .
A caminho do céu?
Mas que céu pode satisfazer teu sonho de céu?

Morrer sem deixar um sulco, um risco, uma sombra,
A lembrança de uma sombra
Em nenhum coração, em nenhum pensamento,
Em nenhuma epiderme.

At its center
the two-chambered shell
in a scarlet sea.
Shell, rose or tamarind?

In the dark hiding place
the springs of life
vainly bleeding
from a double wound.

All well concealed
beneath the guise
of a simple print:
head-on, from the side,
black on white.

CONSUMMATE DEATH

To die.
To die body and soul.
Completely.

To die without leaving the body's sorry remains.
The bloodless wax mask
ringed by flowers
that will—lucky them!—rot in a day,
bathed in tears
born less of grief than fear of death.

To die without leaving by some chance an errant soul . . .
On the road to heaven?
But what heaven could ever satisfy your dream of heaven?

To die without leaving a furrow, a trace, a shadow,
the memory of a shadow
in any heart, in any mind,
in any skin.

Morrer tão completamente
Que um dia ao lerem o teu nome num papel
Perguntem: "Quem foi? . . . "

Morrer mais completamente ainda,
— Sem deixar sequer esse nome.

A ESTRELA

Vi uma estrela tão alta,
Vi uma estrela tão fria!
Vi uma estrela luzindo
Na minha vida vazia.

Era uma estrela tão alta!
Era uma estrela tão fria!
Era uma estrela sozinha
Luzindo no fim do dia.

Por que da sua distância
Para a minha companhia
Não baixava aquela estrela?
Por que tão alta luzia?

E ouvi-a na sombra funda
Responder que assim fazia
Para dar uma esperança
Mais triste ao fim do meu dia.

MOZART NO CÉU

No dia 5 de dezembro de 1791 Wolfgang Amadeus Mozart entrou
          [no céu, como um artista de circo, fazendo piruetas
          [extraordinárias sobre um mirabolante cavalo branco.

To die so completely
that one day on seeing your name on paper
they'll have to ask, "Who was he?" . . .

To die more completely still
—without even leaving so much as that name.

THE STAR

I saw a star so distant,
a star so coldly white,
I saw a star shining
in my empty life.

It was such a cold star!
It shone from so far away.
It was a lone star shining
at the end of day.

Why didn't that star
come down from on high?
Why did it just shine there
far up in the sky?

And I heard it respond
that it shone in that way
to give the saddest hope
to the end of my day.

MOZART IN HEAVEN

On the fifth of December 1791 Wolfgang Amadeus Mozart entered
    heaven like a circus performer, making extravagant
    pirouettes on the back of a dazzling white horse.

Os anjinhos atônitos diziam: Que foi? Que não foi?
Melodias jamais ouvidas voavam nas linhas suplementares
[superiores da pauta.
Um momento se suspendeu a contemplação inefável.
A Virgem beijou-o na testa
E desde então Wolfgang Amadeus Mozart foi o mais moço dos
[anjos.

CANÇÃO DO VENTO E DA MINHA VIDA

O vento varria as folhas,
O vento varria os frutos,
O vento varria as flores . . .
      E a minha vida ficava
      Cada vez mais cheia
      De frutos, de flores, de folhas.

O vento varria as luzes
O vento varria as músicas,
O vento varria os aromas . . .
      E a minha vida ficava
      Cada vez mais cheia
      De aromas, de estrelas, de cânticos.

O vento varria os sonhos
E varria as amizades . . .
O vento varria as mulheres.
      E a minha vida ficava
      Cada vez mais cheia
      De afetos e de mulheres.

O vento varria os meses
E varria os teus sorrisos . . .
O vento varria tudo!
      E a minha vida ficava
      Cada vez mais cheia
      De tudo.

The astonished little angels asked, "What gives? What
    doesn't?"
Never-before-heard melodies soared on lines above the staff.

For a split second the ineffable contemplation ceased.
The Virgin kissed him on the forehead
and from that moment on, Wolfgang Amadeus Mozart was
    the youngest angel.

SONG OF THE WIND AND MY LIFE

The wind swept away the leaves,
The wind swept away the fruit,
The wind swept away the flowers . . .
    And my life became
    ever fuller
    of fruit, of flowers, of leaves.

The wind swept away the lights,
The wind swept away the music,
The wind swept away the perfume . . .
    And my life became
    ever fuller
    of perfume, song, and stars.

The wind swept away dreams,
The wind swept away friendships . . .
The wind swept away women.
    And my life became
    ever fuller
    of women and of love.

The wind swept away the months
and swept away your smiles . . .
The wind swept away all before it!
    And my life became
    fuller, ever fuller
    all the time.

CANÇÃO DA PARADA DO LUCAS

Parada do Lucas
— O trem não parou.

Ah, se o trem parasse
Minha alma incendida
Pediria à Noite
Dois seios intactos.

Parada do Lucas
— O trem não parou.

Ah, se o trem parasse
Eu iria aos mangues
Dormir na escureza
Das águas defuntas.

Parada do Lucas
— O trem não parou.

Nada aconteceu
Senão a lembrança
Do crime espantoso
Que o tempo engoliu.

CANÇÃO DE MUITAS MARIAS

Uma, duas, três Marias,
Tira o pé da noite escura.
Se uma Maria é demais,
Duas, três, que não seria?

SONG OF LUCAS STATION

Lucas Station.
—The train didn't stop.

Ah, if the train were to stop
my blazing soul
would ask the Night
for two perfect breasts.

Lucas Station.
—The train didn't stop.

Ah, if the train were to stop
I would go down to the swamps
and sleep in the darkness
of the stagnant waters.

Lucas Station.
—The train didn't stop.

Nothing happened,
nothing but the memory
of a fearsome crime
time has swallowed.

SONG OF MANY MARIAS

One, two, three Marias,
take your foot out of the night.
If just one Maria's too many,
how can two or three be right?

Uma é Maria da Graça,
Outra é Maria Adelaide:
Uma tem o pai pau-d'água,
Outra tem o pai alcaide.

A terceira é tão distante,
Que só vendo por binóculo.
Essa é Maria das Neves,
Que chora e sofre do fígado!

Há mais Marias na terra.
Tantas que é um não acabar,
—Mais que as estrelas no céu,
Mais que as folhas na floresta,
Mais que as areias no mar!

Por uma saltei de vara,
Por outra estudei tupi.
Mas a melhor das Marias
Foi aquela que eu perdi.

Essa foi a Mária Cândida
(Mária digam por favor),
Minha Maria enfermeira,
Tão forte e morreu de gripe,
Tão pura e não teve sorte,
Maria do meu amor.

E depois dessa Maria,
Que foi cândida no nome,
Cândida no coração;
Que em vida foi a das Dores,
E hoje é Maria do Céu:
Não cantarei mais nenhuma,
Que a minha lira estalou,
Que a minha lira morreu!

One is Maria of Mercy,
Maria Adelaide is the other:
The father of one is a drunkard,
the other, an ugly old bother.

The third Maria's so distant
you need binoculars to see her.
This one's Maria of Snows,
who weeps and endures a bad liver.

This world contains still more Marias.
A million, a billion, still more
—more than stars in the sky,
leaves in the forest,
or grains of sand on the shore!

For one I skipped over a pole,
for another I studied Tupi,
but the very best of Marias
was the one who got away from me.

This one was Maria the Candid
(plain old Maria will do),
my nurse Maria, so healthy
and yet who died of the flu,
so pure and yet so unlucky,
Maria, my love was for you.

And after this Maria
candid in heart
and in name,
who in life was Maria of Sorrows
and today is Maria of the Sky,
I will sing no other Maria,
for my lyre has cracked,
my lyre has died.

RONDÓ DO CAPITÃO

Bão balalão,
Senhor capitão,
Tirai este peso
Do meu coração.
Não é de tristeza,
Não é de aflição:
É só de esperança,
Senhor capitão!
A leve esperança,
A aérea esperança . . .
Aérea, pois não!
— Peso mais pesado
Não existe não.
Ah, livrai-me dele,
Senhor capitão!

ÚLTIMA CANÇÃO DO BECO

Beco que cantei num dístico
Cheio de elipses mentais,
Beco das minhas tristezas,
Das minhas perplexidades
(Mas também dos meus amores,
Dos meus beijos, dos meus sonhos),
Adeus para nunca mais!

Vão demolir esta casa.
Mas meu quarto vai ficar,
Não como forma imperfeita
Neste mundo de aparências:
Vai ficar na eternidade,
Com seus livros, com seus quadros,
Intacto, suspenso no ar!

THE CAPTAIN'S RONDEAU

Diddle dee dee
Captain-and-Chief
cart off this weight,
give my heart some relief!
This weight that's not sadness,
not sadness nor grief,
this weight that's mere hope,
oh Captain-and-Chief!
Hope like a feather,
like air—
Air? What's this?
A weightier weight
doesn't exist.
Oh save me from hope,
mighty Captain-and-Chief!

PARTING SONG FOR THE ALLEY

Alley I sang in a couplet
full of mental ellipses,
alley of my sorrows,
of my fears and doubts
(but also of my loves,
of my kisses, of my dreams),
So long now forever!

They are going to tear down this house
but my room will remain
not like an imperfect form
in this world of appearances
but rather as part of eternity
with its books, its paintings
intact, suspended in the air!

Beco de sarças de fogo,
De paixões sem amanhãs,
Quanta luz mediterrânea
No esplendor da adolescência
Não recolheu nestas pedras
O orvalho das madrugadas,
A pureza das manhãs!

Beco das minhas tristezas.
Não me envergonhei de ti!
Foste rua de mulheres?
Todas são filhas de Deus!
Dantes foram carmelitas . . .
E eras só de pobres quando,
Pobre, vim morar aqui.

Lapa — Lapa do Desterro —,
Lapa que tanto pecais!
(Mas quando bate seis horas,
Na primeira voz dos sinos,
Como na voz que anunciava
A conceição de Maria,
Que graças angelicais!)

Nossa Senhora do Carmo,
De lá de cima do altar,
Pede esmolas para os pobres,
— Para mulheres tão tristes,
Para mulheres tão negras,
Que vêm nas portas do templo
De noite se agasalhar.

Beco que nasceste à sombra
De paredes conventuais,
És como a vida, que é santa
Pesar de todas as quedas.
Por isso te amei constante
E canto para dizer-te
Adeus para nunca mais!

Alley of burning bushes,
of passions with no tomorrow,
how much Mediterranean light
in its youthful glory
collected in these stones
through the dew of dawn,
the clarity of mornings!

Alley of my sorrows.
I was never ashamed of you.
Were you a street of whores?
They too are children of God.
Before that you were home to nuns . . .
and to the poor when
poor myself, I came to live here.

Lapa—Lapa of the exile—
Lapa with your many sins!
(But when six o'clock sounds
in the first voice of the bells,
what angelic grace!
—as in that voice that first told Mary
of Christ's conception.)

From there above the altar,
Our Lady of Carmel
seeks alms for the poor,
—for those women so sad
for those women so dark
who huddle in her doors
at nightfall.

Alley born in the shadow
of convent walls,
you are like life that is sacred
despite its disappointments.
That's why I have always loved you
That's why I sing to you to say
so long, so long forever!

BELO BELO

Belo belo belo,
Tenho tudo quanto quero.

Tenho o fogo de constelações extintas há milênios.
E o risco brevíssimo — que foi? passou! — de tantas estrelas
[cadentes.

A aurora apaga-se,
E eu guardo as mais puras lágrimas da aurora.

O dia vem, e dia adentro
Continuo a possuir o segredo grande da noite.

Belo belo belo,
Tenho tudo quanto quero.

Não quero o êxtase nem os tormentos.
Não quero o que a terra só dá com trabalho.

As dádivas dos anjos são inaproveitáveis:
Os anjos não compreendem os homens.

Não quero amar,
Não quero ser amado.
Não quero combater,
Não quero ser soldado.

— Quero a delícia de poder sentir as coisas mais simples.

LOVELY LOVELY

Lovely lovely lovely,
I have all my heart desires.

I have the fire of constellations extinct now for millennia.
And the briefest flash—What's that?—It's gone!—of so many
    falling stars.

The dawn fades
and I retain its purest tears.

Day breaks and all day long I keep
the night's great secret.

Lovely lovely lovely
I have all my heart desires.

I don't want ecstasy or torment.
I don't want what the earth only yields with sweat.

The gifts of angels are useless:
Angels don't understand human beings.

I don't want to love,
I don't want to be loved.
I don't want to fight,
I don't want to be a soldier.

All I want is the pleasure of being able to experience
    the simplest things.

ACALANTO DE JOHN TALBOT

Dorme, meu filhinho,
Dorme sossegado.
Dorme, que a teu lado
Cantarei baixinho.
O dia não tarda . . .
Vai amanhecer:
Como é frio o ar!
O anjinho da guarda
Que o Senhor te deu,
Pode adormecer,
Pode descansar,
Que te guardo eu.

UBIQÜIDADE

Estás em tudo que penso,
Estás em quanto imagino:
Estás no horizonte imenso,
Estás no grão pequenino.

Estás na ovelha que pasce,
Estás no rio que corre:
Estás em tudo que nasce,
Estás em tudo que morre.

Em tudo estás, nem repousas,
O ser tão mesmo e diverso!
(Eras no início das cousas,
Serás no fim do universo.)

Estás na alma e nos sentidos.
Estás no espírito, estás
Na letra, e, os tempos cumpridos,
No céu, no céu estarás.

LULLABY FOR JOHN TALBOT

Slumber my little one,
peacefully sleep.
Slumber while close by you
I softly sing.
Light's going to break . . .
Dawn won't delay.
What a chill day!
The guardian angel
sent from on high
can nod off,
can rest,
while I watch by your side.

UBIQUITY

You are in all I think
you are in all I dream:
You are in the vast horizon,
you are in the smallest seed.

You are in the sheep that grazes,
the stream that wanders by,
you are in all that's born
in all too that must die.

You are in all things, never resting
—oh being, many and one!
As much in the beginning
as in the end to come.

You are in the soul, the senses,
you are in the spirit, you live
in words and time once over,
you'll live in the sky, you'll live!

PISCINA

Que silêncio enorme!
Na piscina verde
Gorgoleja trépida
A água da carranca.

Só a lua se banha
— Lua gorda e branca —
Na piscina verde.
Como a lua é branca!

Corre um arrepio
Silenciosamente
Na piscina verde:
Lua ela não quer.

Ah o que ela quer
A piscina verde
É o corpo queimado
De certa mulher
Que jamais se banha
Na espadana branca
Da água da carranca.

PARDALZINHO

O pardalzinho nasceu
Livre. Quebraram-lhe a asa.
Sacha lhe deu uma casa,
Água, comida e carinhos.
Foram cuidados em vão:
A casa era uma prisão,
O pardalzinho morreu.
O corpo Sacha enterrou
No jardim; a alma, essa voou
Para o céu dos passarinhos!

POOL

What an enormous silence!
Tremulous in the green pool
the water from the gargoyle
gurgles.

Only the moon
—the plump white moon—
bathes in the green pool.
How white the moon is!

Silently
a shudder ripples
the green pool:
It's not the moon it wants.

Ah, what it wants,
the green pool,
is the sunburned body
of a certain woman
who never bathes
in the white water
from the gargoyle.

SPARROW

The little sparrow was born
free. They broke his wing.
Sacha gave the sparrow a home,
food, love—everything.
All in vain.
The house was jail; the sparrow died.
Sacha buried the body;
the soul no, it could fly!

EU VI UMA ROSA

Eu vi uma rosa
— Uma rosa branca —
Sozinha no galho.
No galho? Sozinha
No jardim, na rua.

Sozinha no mundo.

Em torno, no entanto,
Ao sol de mei-dia,
Toda a natureza
Em formas e cores
E sons esplendia.

Tudo isso era excesso.

A graça essencial,
Mistério inefável
— Sobrenatural —
Da vida e do mundo,
Estava ali na rosa
Sozinha no galho.

Sozinha no tempo.

Tão pura e modesta,
Tão perto do chão,
Tão longe na glória
Da mística altura,
Dir-se-ia que ouvisse
Do arcanjo invisível
As palavras santas
De outra Anunciação.

I SAW A ROSE

I saw a rose
—a white rose—
alone on a branch.
A branch? Alone
in a garden, alone in the street.

Alone in the world.

And yet, around
the midday sun
all nature
shone out
in sounds and shapes and colors.

All this was excess.

The essential grace,
the ineffable mystery
—supernatural—
of life, the world
was present in the rose
alone on the branch.

Alone in time.

So pure and modest,
so near the ground,
so far in the glory
of the mystic heights
you would almost say you could hear
the invisible archangel proclaim
the holy words
of a new Annunciation.

BELO BELO
LOVELY LOVELY
1948

BRISA

Vamos viver no Nordeste, Anarina.
Deixarei aqui meus amigos, meus livros, minhas riquezas, minha
                                                    [vergonha.
Deixarás aqui tua filha, tua avó, teu marido, teu amante.
Aqui faz muito calor.
No Nordeste faz calor também.
Mas lá tem brisa:
Vamos viver de brisa, Anarina.

POEMA SÓ PARA JAIME OVALLE

Quando hoje acordei, ainda fazia escuro
(Embora a manhã já estivesse avançada).
Chovia.
Chovia uma triste chuva de resignação
Como contraste e consolo ao calor tempestuoso da noite.
Então me levantei,
Bebi o café que eu mesmo preparei,
Depois me deitei novamente, acendi um cigarro e fiquei
                                        [pensando . . .
— Humildemente pensando na vida e nas mulheres que amei.

ESCUSA

Eurico Alves, poeta baiano,
Salpicado de orvalho, leite cru e tenro cocô de cabrito,

Sinto muito, mas não posso ir a Feira de Sant'Ana.

Sou poeta da cidade.
Meus pulmões viraram máquinas inumanas e aprenderam a
                [respirar o gás carbônico das salas de cinema.

BREEZE

Let's go live up north, Anarina.
I'll leave my friends, my books, my possessions, my shame.
You'll leave your daughter, your grandmother, your husband,
    your lover.
Here it's very hot.
It's also hot up north.
But there's a breeze:
We'll live there on air, Anarina.

POEM JUST FOR JAIME OVALLE

When I woke up this morning it was still dark
—even though it was already day—
and it was raining.
Raining a sad rain of resignation
as if in contrast to and solace for the night's tempestuous heat.
Then I got up
and drank the coffee I myself prepared,
lay down again, lit up a cigarette and began to think

—humbly to think about life and the women I have loved.

EXCUSE

Eurico Alves, Bahian poet,
spattered with dew, milk straight from the cow and tender
    droppings of baby goats,
I'm very sorry but I can't accept your invitation to Feira de
    Sant'Ana.
I am a city poet.
My lungs have become inhuman machines, they've learned to
    breathe carbon dioxide in movie theaters.

Como o pão que o diabo amassou.
Bebo leite de lata.
Falo com A., que é ladrão.
Aperto a mão de B., que é assassino.
Há anos que não vejo romper o sol, que não lavo os olhos nas
                                        [cores das madrugadas.

Eurico Alves, poeta baiano,
Não sou mais digno de respirar o ar puro dos currais da roça.

TEMA E VOLTAS

Mas para quê
Tanto sofrimento,
Se nos céus há o lento
Deslizar da noite?

Mas para quê
Tanto sofrimento,
Se lá fora o vento
É um canto na noite?

Mas para quê
Tanto sofrimento,
Se agora, ao relento,
Cheira a flor da noite?

Mas para quê
Tanto sofrimento,
Se o meu pensamento
É livre na noite?

I eat bread kneaded by the devil.
I drink canned milk.
I talk with A, a thief,
shake hands with B, a murderer.
It's been years now since I've seen a sunrise, since I've bathed
    my eyes in the colors of the dawn.

Eurico Alves, Bahian poet,
I'm no longer fit to breathe the fresh air of your country
    barnyards.

THEMES AND VARIATIONS

But why
so much suffering
if the skies see
the slow slide of the night?

But why
so much suffering
if there outside the wind
is a song in the night?

But why
so much suffering
if the moist air is now fragrant
with the flower of night?

But why
so much suffering
if my mind is free to wander
in the night?

CANTO DE NATAL

O nosso menino
Nasceu em Belém.
Nasceu tão-somente
Para querer bem.

Nasceu sobre as palhas
O nosso menino.
Mas a mãe sabia
Que ele era divino.

Vem para sofrer
A morte na cruz,
O nosso menino.
Seu nome é Jesus.

Por nós ele aceita
O humano destino:
Louvemos a glória
De Jesus menino.

TEMPO-SERÁ

A Eternidade está longe
(Menos longe que o estirão
Que existe entre o meu desejo.
E a palma de minha mão).

Um dia serei feliz?
Sim, mas não há de ser já:
A Eternidade está longe,
Brinca de tempo-será.

CHRISTMAS SONG

Our child was born
far over the sea,
born for one purpose
—to love you and me.

He was born in the straw,
our little child
but his mother knew
he had come from on high.

He came here to suffer
the cross's pain,
our little child,
Jesus by name.

For us he embraces
the sorrows of this life.
All praise and all glory
to the child Christ!

HIDE-AND-SEEK

Eternity is far off
(and yet, it's less far than
the length between my longing
and the palm of my hand).

Will I one day be happy?
Yes, but not now, you see.
Still far off, Eternity
plays hide-and-seek with me.

A MÁRIO DE ANDRADE AUSENTE

Anunciaram que você morreu.
Meus olhos, meus ouvidos testemunham:
A alma profunda, não.
Por isso não sinto agora a sua falta.

Sei bem que ela virá
(Pela força persuasiva do tempo).
Virá súbito um dia,
Inadvertida para os demais.
Por exemplo assim:
À mesa conversarão de uma coisa e outra,
Uma palavra lançada à toa
Baterá na franja dos lutos de sangue,
Alguém perguntará em que estou pensando,
Sorrirei sem dizer que em você
Profundamente.

Mas agora não sinto a sua falta.

(É sempre assim quando o ausente
Partiu sem se despedir:
Você não se despediu.)

Você não morreu: ausentou-se.
Direi: Faz tempo que ele não escreve.
Irei a São Paulo: você não virá ao meu hotel.
Imaginarei: Está na chacrinha de São Roque.
Saberei que não, você ausentou-se. Para outra vida?

A vida é uma só. A sua continua
Na vida que você viveu.
Por isso não sinto agora a sua falta.

TO MÁRIO DE ANDRADE, ABSENT

They announced you had died.
My eyes, my ears took in the fact.
But not my heart.
That's why right now I don't miss you.

I know I will
(time is persuasive)
I'll feel it suddenly one day
without anyone being the wiser.
For example,
they'll be talking about something or other over dinner.
A casual word
will touch the fringes of mourning for one of the family.
Someone will ask what I'm thinking
and I'll smile without hinting
my mind is on you, wholly on you.

Still, right now I don't miss you.

(It's always like that when the absent one
leaves without saying good-bye.
You didn't say good-bye.)

You didn't die: you went away.
I'll say, "He hasn't written for a while now."
I'll go to São Paulo. You won't visit me at my hotel.
I'll tell myself, "He's at the country house in São Roque."
And I'll know it isn't true, I'll know you've left.
　　Left for another life?
Life is just life. Your life goes on
within this life you lived.
That's why right now I don't miss you.

BELO BELO

Belo belo minha bela
Tenho tudo que não quero
Não tenho nada que quero
Não quero óculos nem tosse
Nem obrigação de voto
Quero quero
Quero a solidão dos píncaros
A água da fonte escondida
A rosa que floresceu
Sobre a escarpa inaccessível
A luz da primeira estrela
Piscando no lusco-fusco
Quero quero
Quero dar a volta ao mundo
Só num navio de vela
Quero rever Pernambuco
Quero ver Bagdá e Cusco
Quero quero
Quero o moreno de Estela
Quero a brancura de Elisa
Quero a saliva de Bela
Quero as sardas de Adalgisa
Quero quero tanta coisa
Belo belo
Mas basta de lero-lero
Vida noves fora zero.

LOVELY LOVELY

Lovely lovely, my lovely
I have everything I don't want
I have nothing I want.
I don't want eyeglasses, a cough
or the obligation to vote
I want I want
I want the solitude of summits
the water of the hidden spring
the rose that bloomed
beneath the inaccessible slope
I want the first star light, star bright
winking in the twilight
I want I want
I want to circle the world
all alone in a sailboat
I want to revisit Pernambuco
I want to see Baghdad and Cuzco
I want I want
I want Estela's darkness
the whiteness of Elisa
I want Bela's saliva
the freckles of Adalgisa
I want I want so many things
Lovely lovely
But enough jibber-jabber—
Life's a zero—that's all that matters.

NEOLOGISMO

Beijo pouco, falo menos ainda.
Mas invento palavras
Que traduzem a ternura mais funda
E mais cotidiana.
Inventei, por exemplo, o verbo teadorar.
Intransitivo:
Teadoro, Teodora.

A REALIDADE E A IMAGEM

O arranha-céu sobe no ar puro lavado pela chuva
E desce refletido na poça de lama do pátio.
Entre a realidade e a imagem, no chão seco que as separa,

Quatro pombas passeiam.

POEMA PARA SANTA ROSA

Pousa na minha a tua mão, protonotária.
O alexandrino, ainda que sem a cesura mediana, aborrece-me.
Depois, eu mesmo já escrevi: Pousa a mão na minha testa.
E Raimundo Correia: "Pousa aqui, pousa ali, etc."
É Pouso demais. Basta Pouso Alto.
Tão distante e tão presente. Como uma reminiscência da infância.

NEOLOGISM

I kiss very little, talk still less
but I invent words
that express a tenderness
of the deepest, most everyday sort.
I've invented, for instance, the verb "to you-adore."
Intransitive:
I you-adore, my Eudora.

REALITY AND IMAGE

The skyscraper rises in the clear air rinsed by rain
and descends reflected in the mud puddle in the courtyard.
Between reality and image, on the dry ground that divides
    the two,
Four pigeons go for a stroll.

POEM FOR SAINT ROSE

Rest your hand in mine, prothonotary.
The alexandrine, even without caesura, annoys me.
And besides, even I once wrote, "Rest your hand on my forehead."
And Raimundo Correia, "Rest it here, rest it there, etc."
It's entirely too much Resting. Mountain Rest is quite enough.
So distant and so close at hand, like a childhood memory.

Pousa na minha a tua mão, protonotária.
Gosto de "protonotária".
Me lembra meu pai.
E pinta bem a quem eu quero.
Sei que ela vai perguntar: — O que é protonotária?
Responderei:
— Protonotário é o dignitário da Cúria Romana que expede, nas
                    [grandes causas, os atos que os simples notários
                            [apostólicos expedem nas pequenas.
E ela: — Será o Benedito?

— Meu bem, minha ternura é um fato, mas não gosta de
                                        [se mostrar:
É dentuça e dissimulada.
Santa Rosa me compreende.

Pousa na minha a tua mão, protonotária.

CÉU

A criança olha
Para o céu azul.
Levanta a mãozinha,
Quer tocar o céu.

Não sente a criança
Que o céu é ilusão:
Crê que o não alcança,
Quando o tem na mão.

Rest your hand in mine, prothonotary.
I like the word "prothonotary."
It reminds me of my father.
And it's a good description of the one I love.
I know she's going to ask, "So what's a prothonotary?"
And I'll explain:
> "A prothonotary is the official of the Roman Curia who
> dispatches the documents in important matters dispatched by
> regular apostolic notaries on lesser occasions.
And she'll say, "Are you crazy?"

My love, my feeling for you is real but it doesn't like
    to show itself:
It's bucktoothed and dissembling.
You know what I mean, Saint Rose.

Rest your hand in mine, prothonotary.

SKY

The child looks up
at the blue beyond,
straining to cup it
in a small palm.

The sky's an illusion
he can't understand.
He thinks beyond reach
what's already in hand.

REPOSTA A VINÍCIUS

Poeta sou; pai, pouco; irmão, mais.
Lúcido, sim; eleito, não.
E bem triste de tantos ais
Que me enchem a imaginação.

Com que sonho? Não sei bem não.
Talvez com me bastar, feliz
— Ah feliz como jamais fui! —,
Arrancando do coração
— Arrancando pela raiz —
Este anseio infinito e vão
De possuir o que me possui.

O BICHO

Vi ontem um bicho
Na imundície do pátio
Catando comida entre os detritos.

Quando achava alguma coisa,
Não examinava nem cheirava:
Engolia com voracidade.

O bicho não era um cão,
Não era um gato,
Não era um rato.

O bicho, meu Deus, era um homem.

REPLY TO VINÍCIUS

Poet I am; father, just a little; brother, a bit more.
I'm lucid, yes, but not a genius.
And I'm weary of these "Woe-Is-Mes"
that crowd my mind.

Of what do I dream? I really couldn't say.
Perhaps of being self-sufficient, happy
—happy like I never was!—
Of yanking from my heart
—of yanking out by the root—
this vain and ceaseless yearning
to possess what possesses me.

THE CREATURE

Yesterday I saw a creature
amidst the garbage in the courtyard,
hunting for food amidst the debris.

When it found something
it didn't look or smell
—just wolfed it down.

The creature wasn't a dog
or a cat
or a rat.

The creature, my God, was a man.

O RIO

Ser como o rio que deflui
Silencioso dentro da noite.
Não temer as trevas da noite.
Se há estrelas nos céus, refleti-las.
E se os céus se pejam de nuvens,
Como o rio as nuvens são água,
Refleti-las também sem mágoa
Nas profundidades tranqüilas.

PRESEPE

Chorava o menino.

Para a mãe, coitada,
Jesus pequenito,
De qualquer maneira
(Mães o sabem . . .), era
Das entranhas dela
O fruto bendito.
José, seu marido,
Ah esse aceitava,
Carpinteiro simples,
O que Deus mandava.
Conhecia o filho
A que vinha neste
Mundo tão bonito,
Tão mal habitado?
Não que ele temesse
O humano flagício:
O fel e o vinagre,
Escárnios, açoites,
O lenho nos ombros,
A lança na ilharga,
A morte na cruz.

THE RIVER

To be like the river that flows on
silent in the night.
Not to fear the dark.
If there are stars, to mirror them.
And if the sky fills with clouds
(after all, they're water too)
to reflect them without sorrow
in its calm depths.

MANGER SCENE

The child cried.

For his mother, poor thing,
baby Jesus
was in any case
(mothers know . . .)
the blessed fruit
of her womb.
Joseph, her husband
ah he—a simple carpenter—
accepted the will of God.
Did the child realize
what awaited him
in this world, so lovely,
so unloving?
Not that he feared
human suffering,
the vinegar, the gall,
insults, lashes,
the wood upon his back,
the lance in his side,
death on the cross.
What frightened him

Mais do que tudo isso
O amedrontaria
A dor de ser homem,
O horror de ser homem,
—Esse bicho estranho
Que desarrazoa
Muito presumido
De sua razão;
—Esse bicho estranho
Que se agita em vão;
Que tudo deseja
Sabendo que tudo
É o mesmo que nada;
—Esse bicho estranho
Que tortura os que ama;
Que até mata, estúpido,
Ao seu semelhante
No ilusivo intento
De fazer o bem!
Os anjos cantavam
Que o menino viera
Para redimir
O homem — essa absurda
Imagem de Deus!
Mas o jumentinho,
Tão manso e calado
Naquele inefável,
Divino momento,
Esse bem sabia
Que inútil seria
Todo o sofrimento
No Sinédrio, no horto,
Nos cravos da cruz;
Que inútil seria
O fel e vinagre
Do bestial flagício;
Ele bem sabia
Que seria inútil
O maior milagre;
Que inútil seria
Todo sacrifício . . .

more than all this
was the pain of being human
—this strange being, man
who talks nonsense
firmly convinced
he is talking perfect sense.
—This strange beast
who flails about in vain
who desires everything
knowing that nothing
really matters.
—This strange creature
who tortures those he loves
who even stupidly kills
his brother
in the deluded hope
of doing good.
The angels sang
that the child had come
to redeem man
—that ludicrous
image of God!
But the little donkey,
so gentle and quiet
in that ineffable,
divine moment,
the donkey knew full well
the futility of all this suffering
in the Sanhedrin, in the garden,
on the nails of the cross,
the futility
of the vinegar and gall
of the savage flagellation;
He knew full well
the futility
of the greatest miracle,
the futility
of every sacrifice.

NOVA POÉTICA

Vou lançar a teoria do poeta sórdido.
Poeta sórdido:
Aquele em cuja poesia há a marca suja da vida.
Vai um sujeito,
Sai um sujeito de casa com a roupa de brim branco muito
                [bem engomada, e na primeira esquina
                [passa um caminhão, salpica-lhe o paletó
                [ou a calça de uma nódoa de lama:
É a vida.

O poema deve ser como a nódoa no brim:
Fazer o leitor satisfeito de si dar o desespero.

Sei que a poesia é também orvalho.
Mas este fica para as menininhas, as estrelas alfas, as virgens cem
                [por cento e as amadas que envelheceram
                [sem maldade.

UNIDADE

Minh'alma estava naquele instante
Fora de mim longe muito longe

Chegaste
E desde logo foi verão
O verão com as suas palmas os seus mormaços os seus ventos
                [de sôfrega mocidade
Debalde os teus afagos insinuavam quebranto e molície
O instinto de penetração já despertado
Era como uma seta de fogo

NEW POETICS

I'm going to launch the theory of the perverse poet.
Perverse poet:
He in whose poetry there is the dirty mark of life.
Here you have a man like any other:
A man like any other leaves the house in his well-starched
     sailcloth suit and at the first corner a truck goes by and
     spatters the pants or jacket with mud:

That's life.

A poem should be like mud on cloth:
It should drive the complacent reader wild.

I know that poetry is also dew.
But this is for good little girls, the brightest stars, virgins
     a hundred percent virgin, and former sweethearts
     who manage to grow old without a hint of malice.

UNION

My soul was in that instant
outside me, far off, very far

You arrived
and suddenly it was summer,
summer with its palm trees, sultry haze, its winds of restless
     youth.
In vain your kisses suggested lethargy, exhaustion.
Once aroused, my instinct
was like a fiery arrow

Foi então que minh'alma veio vindo
Veio vindo de muito longe
Veio vindo
Para de súbito entrar-me violenta e sacudir-me todo
No momento fugaz da unidade.

ARTE DE AMAR

Se queres sentir a felicidade de amar, esquece a tua alma.
A alma é que estraga o amor.
Só em Deus ela pode encontrar satisfação.
Não noutra alma.
Só em Deus — ou fora do mundo.

As almas são incomunicáveis.

Deixa o teu corpo entender-se com outro corpo.

Porque os corpos se entendem, mas as almas não.

AS TRÊS MARIAS

Atrás destas moitas,
Nos troncos, no chão,
Vi, traçado a sangue,
O signo-salmão!

Há larvas, há lêmures
Atrás destas moitas.
Mulas-sem-cabeça,
Visagens afoitas.

It was then my soul came coming
came coming from afar
came coming
to suddenly, violently, enter and shake me to the core
in the fleeting moment of union.

ART OF LOVING

If you want to experience the joy of loving, forget about your soul.
It's the soul that spoils love.
Only in God can it find satisfaction.
Not in another soul.
Only in God—or in some other world.

Souls are not communicable.

Let your body reach an understanding with another body.

Because bodies understand each other but souls, never.

THE THREE MARYS

Behind these thickets,
on the tree trunks, on the ground,
I saw traced out in blood
the Sign of Solomon.

There are larvae, there are lemurs
behind these thickets.
Headless mules,
audacious faces.

Atrás destas moitas
Veio a Moura-Torta
Comer as mãozinhas
Da menina morta!

Há bruxas luéticas
Atrás destas moitas,
Segredando à aragem
Amorosas coitas.

Atrás destas moitas
Vi um rio de fundas
Aguas deletérias,
Paradas, imundas!

Atrás destas moitas . . .
— Que importa? Irei vê-las?
Regiões mais sombrias
Conheço. Sou poeta,
Dentro d'alma levo,
Levo três estrelas,
Levo as três Marias!

INFÂNCIA

Corrida de ciclistas.
Só me lembro de um bambual debruçado no rio.
Três anos?
Foi em Petrópolis.

Procuro mais longe em minhas reminiscências.
Quem me dera recordar a teta negra de minh'ama-de leite . . .
    . . . meus olhos não conseguem romper os ruços definitivos
                                        [do tempo.

Ainda em Petrópolis . . . um pátio de hotel . . . brinquedos
                                        [pelo chão . . .

Behind these thickets
the Hunchback Mooress came
to gobble down the small hands
of the dead girl.

There are syphilitic witches
behind these thickets
murmuring to the breezes
of their unhappy days.

Behind these thickets
I saw a river full of deep
and dangerous waters
—filthy, stagnant!

Behind these thickets . . .
—But what of it? Will I ever see them?
There are yet darker regions
I've known. I am a poet and I carry
in my soul, I carry
the three stars, I carry
the three Marys!

CHILDHOOD

Bicycle race.
I remember nothing but a bamboo grove curved over the stream.
Was I three years old?
This was in Petrópolis.

I forage deeper amidst memories.
How I would like to remember the black teat of my wet nurse . . .
. . . but my eyes can't pierce the perennial fog of time.

Still in Petrópolis . . . a hotel courtyard . . . toys strewn about the
    floor . . .

Depois a casa de São Paulo.
Miguel Guimarães, alegre, míope e mefistofélico,
Tirando reloginhos de plaquê da concha de minha orelha.
O urubu pousado no muro do quintal.
Fabrico uma trombeta de papel.
Comando . . .
O urubu obedece.
Fujo, aterrado do meu primeiro gesto de magia.

Depois . . . a praia de Santos . . .
Corridas em círculos riscados na areia . . .
Outra vez Miguel Guimarães, juiz de chegada, com os seus
                                                    [presentinhos.

A ratazana enorme apanhada na ratoeira.
Outro bambual . . .
O que inspirou a meu irmão a seu único poema:
          "Eu ia por um caminho,
          Encontrei um maracatu.
          O qual vinha direitinho
          Pelas flechas de um bambu."

As marés de equinócio.
O jardim submerso . . .
Meu tio Cláudio erguendo do chão uma ponta de mastro
                                                    [destroçado.
Poesia dos naufrágios!

Depois Petrópolis novamente.
Eu, junto do tanque, de linha amarrada no incisivo de leite,
                                            [sem coragem de puxar.

Véspera de Natal . . . Os chinelinhos atrás da porta . . .
E a manhã seguinte, na cama, deslumbrado com os brinquedos
                                            [trazidos pela fada.

E a chácara da Gávea?
E a casa da Rua Don'Ana?

Later the house in São Paulo.
Miguel Guimarães, lighthearted, myopic, devilish,
suddenly pulling out a tin watch from my ear.
A buzzard, perched there on the garden wall.
I make a paper trumpet,
sound a command . . .
The buzzard obeys.
And I scurry off in fright at my first magic sign.

Later . . . Santos beach . . .
Races in circles traced in sand . . .
Again Miguel Guimarães, finish line judge, with his little
    prizes.

The huge rat in the trap.
Another bamboo grove . . .
inspiration for my brother's one and only poem:
    "I was going down the road
    when I saw the Carnival brass.
    The players marched straight through the bamboo
    before falling on their . . . "

High tides of the equinox.
The flooded garden . . .
Uncle Cláudio picking up the tip of a shattered mast.

Poetry of shipwrecks!

Later, once more in Petrópolis,
myself beside the wash tank, a string looped about a baby tooth
    but lacking the heart to pull.

Christmas Eve . . .   The little slippers behind the door . . .
and next morning, in bed, dazzled by the toys left by the fairy.

And the country house in Gávea?
The house on Don'Ana Street—

Boy, o primeiro cachorro.
Não haveria outro nome depois
(Em casa até as cadelas se chamavam Boy).

Medo de gatunos . . .
Para mim eram homens com cara de pau.

A volta a Pernambuco!
Descoberta dos casarões de telha-vã.
Meu avô materno — um santo . . .
Minha avó batalhadora.

A casa da Rua da União.
O pátio — núcleo de poesia.
O banheiro — núcleo de poesia.
O cambrone — núcleo de poesia (*"la fraicheur des latrines!"*).

A alcova de música — núcleo de mistério.
Tapetinhos de peles de animais.
Ninguém nunca ia lá . . . Silêncio . . . Obscuridade . . .
O piano de armário, teclas amarelecidas, cordas desafinadas.

Descoberta da rua!
Os vendedores a domicílio.
Ai mundo dos papagaios de papel, dos piões, da amarelinha!

Uma noite a menina me tirou da roda de coelho-sai, me levou,
                [imperiosa e ofegante, para um desvão da
                [casa de Dona Aninha Viegas, levantou a
                [sainha e disse mete.

Depois meu avô . . . Descoberta da morte!

Com dez anos vim para o Rio.
Conhecia a vida em suas verdades essenciais.
Estava maduro para o sofrimento
E para a poesia.

Our first dog, Boy.
(There would never be a dog of another name.
In our house even the female dogs would be "Boy.")

Fear of thieves.
For me, they were men with wooden faces.

The return to Pernambuco!
Discovery of the mansions with their red tile roofs.
My mother's father—a saint . . .
My grandmother, a born fighter.

The house on Union Street.
The courtyard—nucleus of poetry.
The bath—nucleus of poetry.
The outhouse—nucleus of poetry ("la fraicheur des latrines!")

The music room—nucleus of mystery.
Little animal skin rugs.
No one ever entered there . . . Silence . . . Darkness . . .
The upright piano with its keys grown yellow and out of tune.

Discovery of the street!
The door-to-door peddlers
Oh that world of paper kites, of spinning tops, of hopscotch!

One night the little girl pulled me away from the circle
    of children playing Rabbit Run. Imperious and panting, she
    took me to a corner of Dona Aninha Viegas's house,
    then raised her little skirt and said, "Stick it here!"

Later my grandfather . . . Discovery of death!

At the age of ten I returned to Rio.
I had become familiar with life's most essential truths.
I was ripe for suffering
and for poetry.

OPUS 10
OPUS 10
1952

BOI MORTO

Como em turvas águas de enchente,
Me sinto a meio submergido
Entre destroços do presente
Dividido, subdividido,
Onde rola, enorme, o boi morto,

Boi morto, boi morto, boi morto.

Árvores da paisagem calma,
Convosco — altas, tão marginais! —
Fica a alma, a atônita alma,
Atônita para jamais.
Que o corpo, esse vai com o boi morto,

Boi morto, boi morto, boi morto.

Boi morto, boi descomedido,
Boi espantosamente, boi
Morto, sem forma ou sentido
Ou significado. O que foi
Ninguém sabe. Agora é boi morto,

Boi morto, boi morto, boi morto.

O GRILO

— Grilo, toca aí um solo de flauta.
— De flauta? Você me acha com cara de flautista?
— A flauta é um belo instrumento. .Não gosta?
— *Troppo dolce!*

DEAD OX

As in muddy floodwaters
I feel myself half-submerged
amidst the rubble of the present
divided, subdivided where, enormous,
the dead ox rolls from side to side.

Dead ox, dead ox, dead ox.

Trees of the calm landscape,
with you—tall and so completely marginal!—
remains the soul, the astonished soul,
forever astonished
because the body goes with the dead ox.

Dead ox, dead ox, dead ox.

Dead ox, enormously ox,
astoundingly ox, without feeling, form
or any meaning. What it once was
nobody knows. Now it is only a dead ox.

Dead ox, dead ox, dead ox.

CRICKET

Cricket, play a solo on your flute.
—"What flute? Do I look like a flutist?"
—The flute is a lovely instrument. Don't you like it?
—"*Troppo dolce!*"

VOZES NA NOITE

Cloc cloc cloc . . .
Saparia no brejo?
Não, são os quatro cãezinhos policiais bebendo água.

POEMA ENCONTRADO POR THIAGO DE MELLO NO *ITINERÁRIO DE PASÁRGADA*

Venus luzia sobre nós tão grande,
Tão intensa, tão bela, que chegava
A parecer escandalosa, e dava
        Vontade de morrer.

RETRATO

O sorriso escasso,
O riso-sorriso,
A risada nunca.
(Como quem consigo
Traz o sentimento
Do madrasto mundo.)

Com os braços colados
Ao longo do corpo,
Vai pela cidade
Grande e cafajeste,
Com o mesmo ar esquivo
Que escolheu nascendo
Na esquiva Itabira.

VOICES IN THE NIGHT

Glup glup glup . . .
Toad chorus in the swamp?
No, just four small police dogs lapping water.

POEM DISCOVERED BY THIAGO DE MELLO IN *ITINERARY OF PASÁRGADA*

Venus shone down on us so vast,
so intense, so beautiful
that it verged on the scandalous
       and made us want to die.

PORTRAIT

The rare smile.
The half-laugh more like a smile
and never really laughter.
(Like one who carries with him
the awareness
of a stepmother world.)

Arms glued
to either side,
you move through the city
vulgar and sublime
with the same air of aloofness
you chose by being born
in aloof Itabira.

Aprendeu com ela
Os olhos metálicos
Com que vê as coisas:
Sem ódio, sem ênfase,
Às vezes com náusea.

Ferro de Itabira,
Em cujos recessos
Um vedor, um dia,
Um vedor — o neto —
Descobriu infante
As fundas nascentes,
O veio, o remanso
Da escusa ternura.

OS NOMES

Duas vezes se morre:
Primeiro na carne, depois no nome.
A carne desaparece, o nome persiste mas
Esvaziando-se de seu casto conteúdo
— Tantos gestos, palavras, silêncios —
Até que um dia sentimos,
Com uma pancada de espanto (ou de remoros?),
Que o nome querido já nos soa como os outros.

Santinha nunca foi para mim o diminutivo de Santa.
Nem Santa nunca foi para mim a mulher sem pecado.
Santinha eram dois olhos míopes, quatro incisivos claros à flor
                                                [da boca.
Era a intuição rápida, o medo de tudo, um certo modo de dizer
                                        ["Meu Deus, valei-me".

The metallic eyes
through which you observe the world
learned with Itabira to see
without hatred or expression,
sometimes with revulsion.

Iron of Itabira
in whose recesses
a prospector, one day,
a prospector—the grandson—
discovered early on
the deep springs,
the vein, the calm
of hidden love.

NAMES

We all die twice:
first the flesh and then the name.
The flesh disappears, the name lives on but
slowly losing its chaste content.
—So many gestures, words, and silences—
until one day we realize
with a shock of surprise (perhaps remorse?)
that the beloved name now sounds like all the rest.

Santinha was never for me simply a diminutive
nor was Santa the name for a woman without sin.
Santinha was two nearsighted eyes, four white teeth up against
      the lip,
swift intuition, fearfulness, a certain way of saying
      "Good Lord, help me!"

Adelaide não foi para mim Adelaide somente,
Mas Cabeleira de Berenice, Inominata, Cassiopéia.
Adelaide hoje apenas substantivo próprio feminino.

Os epitáfios também se apagam, bem sei.
Mais lentamente, porém, do que as reminiscências
Na carne, menos inviolável do que a pedra dos túmulos.

CONSOADA

Quando a Indesejada das gentes chegar
(Não sei se dura ou caroável),
Talvez eu tenha medo.
Talvez sorria, ou diga:
                    — Alô, iniludível!
O meu dia foi bom, pode a noite descer.
(A noite com os seus sortilégios.)
Encontrará lavrado o campo, a casa limpa,
A mesa posta,
Com cada coisa em seu lugar.

LUA NOVA

Meu novo quarto
Virado para o nascente:
Meu quarto, de novo a cavaleiro da entrada da barra.

Depois de dez anos de pátio
Volto a tomar conhecimento da aurora.
Volto a banhar meus olhos no mênstruo incruento das ma-
                                        [drugadas.

Adelaide wasn't simply "Adelaide"
but a host of stars—Bernice's Hair, Inominata, Cassiopeia . . .
Today Adelaide is just a woman's name.

Epitaphs also fade, as I well know
—though more slowly than memories
recorded in the flesh, less inviolable than tombstones.

LATE SUPPER

When the Uninvited One arrives
(forbidding or almost tender, I don't know)
maybe I'll be afraid.
Maybe I'll smile or say:
                         —"Hello there, Inescapable!
My day was good, now night can come."
(The night with its enchantments.)
She will find the fields well tended,
the table set,
and each thing in its right place.

NEW MOON

My new room
facing east:
My room, once more high above the entrance to the harbor.

After ten years of inner courtyards
I am becoming reacquainted with the dawn.
I am beginning again to bathe my eyes in the bloodless flow
        of sunrise.

Todas as manhãs o aeroporto em frente me dá lições de partir:

Hei de aprender com ele
A partir de uma vez
— Sem medo,
Sem remorsos,
Sem saudade.

Não pensem que estou aguardando a lua cheia
— Esse sol da demência
Vaga e noctâmbula.
O que eu mais quero,
O de que preciso
É de lua nova.

Every morning the airport across the way gives me lessons
    in departure.

I shall learn with it
to leave once and for all
—without fear,
without remorse,
without nostalgia.

Don't think I am awaiting the full moon
—that sun of vague,
noctambular madness.
What I most want,
what I most need
is a new moon.

ESTRELA DA TARDE
EVENING STAR
1960

SATÉLITE

Fim de tarde.
No céu plúmbeo
A Lua baça
Paira
Muito cosmograficamente
Satélite.

Desmetaforizada,
Desmitificada,
Despojada do velho segredo de melancolia,
Não é agora o golfão de cismas,
O astro dos loucos e dos enamorados.
Mas tão somente
Satélite.

Ah Lua deste fim de tarde,
Demissionária de atribuições românticas,
Sem show para as disponibilidades sentimentais!

Fatigado de mais-valia,
Gosto de ti assim:
Coisa em si,
— Satélite.

OVALLE

Estavas bem mudado.
Como se tivesses posto aquelas barbas brancas
Para entrar com maior decoro a Eternidade.

SATELLITE

Tail end of afternoon.
In the leaden sky
the tarnished Moon
floats
very cosmographically
satellite.

Demetaphorized,
demythified,
stripped of the old secret of melancholy
and no longer gulf of reveries,
star of madmen and lovers,
but only, so only
satellite.

Ah, Moon of this late afternoon
having walked out on your romantic duties
without any show for sentimental dispositions.

Weary of hyperbole,
I like you just this way:
yourself, yourself alone
—satellite.

OVALLE

You'd changed a lot.
It's as if you'd put on that white beard
to make a more distinguished entrance into Eternity.

Nada de nós te interessava agora.
Calavas sereno e grave
Como no fundo foste sempre
Sob as fantasias verbais enormes
Que faziam rir os teus amigos e
Punham bondade no coração dos maus.

O padre orava:
— "O coro de todos os anjos te receba . . . "
Pensei comigo:
Cantando "Estrela brilhante
Lá do alto-mar! . . . "

Levamos-te cansado ao teu último endereço.
Vi com prazer
Que um dia afinal seremos vizinhos.
Conversaremos longamente
De sepultura a sepultura
No silêncio das madrugadas
Quando o orvalho pingar sem ruído
E o luar for uma coisa só.

LETRA PARA HEITOR DOS PRAZERES

— Juriti-pepena
    Tão perto do fim . . .
— Grande é minha pena,
    Nem há outra assim!
— Juriti-pepena,
    Qual é tua pena?
    Conta para mim!
— Não posso, me'irmão,
    Que ela está lá dentro,
    Muito lá no fundo
    De meu coração.

Nothing about us interested you now.
You remained solemnly, serenely silent
as you had always been deep down
beneath the fantastic wordplays
that made your friends laugh
and softened the hardhearted.

The priest prayed:
—"May the angelic chorus receive you . . . "
and I thought
"May they receive you singing 'Radiant Star
of the High Sea'!" . . .

We brought you, weary, to your last address.
I noted with pleasure
that we will one day be neighbors.
We'll talk at length
grave to grave
in the silence of the dawn
when the dew drips noiselessly
and the moon beams down a single sheet of light.

LYRICS FOR HEITOR DOS PRAZERES

Wild dove, wild dove
your end is so near . . .
—My pain is enormous,
none other's so severe!
—Wild dove, wild dove,
what pain can this be?
Tell me all about it,
explain your pain to me.
—I can't do that, brother,
my pain lies down too far
—in the very deepest
reaches of my heart.

— Juriti-pepena,
  É pena de amor?
— Não, é de paixão.
— Ah, agora te entendo:
  Não há maior pena.
  Pobre, pobre, pobre
  Juriti-pepena!

VERSOS PARA JOAQUIM

Joaquim, a vontade do Senhor é às vezes difícil de aceitar.
Tanto Simeão desejoso de ouvir o celeste chamado!
Por que então chamar a que estava apenas a meio de sua
                                      [tarefa?

A indispensável?
A insubstituível?
(Por isso sorri com lágrimas quando te vi, antes da missa,
    [ajeitar o laço de fita nos cabelos de tua caçulinha.)

Ah, bem sei, Joaquim, que o teu coração é tão grande quanto o da
                                     [mãe melhor.
Mas que tristeza! Ela foi demais, estou de mal com Deus.
— Joaquim, a vontade do Senhor é às vezes inaceitável.

ANTÔNIA

Amei Antônia de maneira insensata.
Antônia morava numa casa que para mim não era casa, era
                                     [um empíreo.

Mas os anos foram passando.
Os anos são inexoráveis.
Antônia morreu.
A casa em que Antônia morava foi posta abaixo.

—Wild dove, wild dove,
is your pain the pain of love?
—No, the pain of passion.
—Not another word!
There's no pain more painful
poor, poor little bird.

POEM FOR JOAQUIM

Joaquim, the will of the Lord is sometimes hard to accept.
So many Simons eager to hear the heavenly call!
Why then summon home a woman whose work was only half
    done?

Someone indispensable?
Someone irreplaceable?
(That's why I smiled through tears when I saw you before mass
    fixing the ribbon in your youngest's hair.)

Oh I know, Joaquim, your heart is big as that of the best mother.

But how sad! It's just too much, I'm no longer friends with God.
—Joaquim, the will of the Lord is sometimes unacceptable.

ANTÔNIA

I loved Antônia madly.
Antônia lived in a house that for me wasn't a house
    but the highest heaven.

Still, the years kept passing.
The years are merciless.
Antônia died.
They tore down the house in which Antônia used to live.

Eu mesmo já não sou aquele que amou Antônia e que Antônia
                                          [não amou.

Aliás, previno, muito humildemente, que isto não é crônica nem
                                          [poema.
É apenas
Uma nova versão, a mais recente, do tema *ubi sunt*,
Que dedico, ofereço e consagro
A meu dileto amigo Augusto Meyer.

PASSEIO EM SÃO PAULO

Saio de hotel com quatro olhos,
— Dois do presente,
Dois do passado.
Anhangabaú que já não é *dos suicídios passionais!*
O Hotel Esplanada virou catacumba.
Enfim a Rua Direita!
A minha Rua Direita!
Que saudades tinha dela!
Ainda existe a Casa Kosmos, mas
Não tem impermeáveis em liquidação.
Praça Antônio Prado, onde
Tudo é novo, salvo aquela meia dúzia de sobradinhos.
Montanha-russa de Avenida São João!
O *anjo cor-de-rosa* não é mais cor-de-rosa:
O tempo patinou-o de negro.
Almoço com Di,
Que hoje é Emiliano di Cavalcanti.
Volto ao hotel pelo Anhangabaú.
Onde as *Juvenilidades auriverdes?* Onde
A passiflora? o espanto? a loucura? o desejo?
Ubi sunt?
Ubi sum?
— Obrigado, Mário, pela tua companhia.

And I myself am no longer the one who loved Antônia and
　　Antônia didn't love.

Moreover, I very humbly warn you that this isn't a story or poem.

It's just
one more version—the most recent—of the old *ubi sunt* theme
that I offer, dedicate, devote
to my dear friend, Augusto Meyer.

A WALK THROUGH SÃO PAULO

I leave the hotel with four eyes,
—two on the present,
two on the past.
Anhangabaú, no longer the setting for *lovelorn suicides*.
The Hotel Esplanade now a catacomb.
Finally Straight Street,
dear old crooked Straight Street!
How I'd missed you!
The Kosmos Store is still there but
"We have no raincoats on sale."
Antônio Prado Square where
everything is new except for a half-dozen little two-story houses.
The roller coaster of Saint John Avenue!
The pink angel no longer pink
(time has coated him with a black film.)
I lunch with Di
who is today Emiliano di Cavalcanti.
I return to the hotel via Anhangabaú.
Where are the *Gilt-Green Youth?* What has become
of *the passionflower? the fear? the madness? the desire?*
Ubi sunt?
Ubi sum?
—Thanks, Mário, for your company.

EMBALO

No balanço das águas,
Ao trépido pulsar
Da máquina, embalar
As persistentes mágoas
Das peremptas feridas . . .
Beber o céu nos ventos
Sabendo a sonolentos
Sais e iodados relentos.
Anseios de insofridas
Esperas e esperanças
Diluem-se na bruma
Como na vaga a espuma
— Flores de espumas mansas —
Que a um lado e outro abotoa
Da cortadora proa.
Azuis de águas e céus . . .
Sou nada, e entanto agora
Eis-me centro finito
Do círculo infinito
De mar e céus afora.
— Estou onde está Deus.

PEREGRINAÇÃO

Quando olhada de face, era um abril.
Quando olhada de lado, era um agosto.
Duas mulheres numa: tinha o rosto
Gordo de frente, magro de perfil.

Fazia as sobrancelhas com um til;
A boca, como um o (quase). Isto posto,
Não vou dizer o quanto a amei. Nem gosto
De me lembrar, que são tristezas mil.

ROCKING SONG

In the rolling motion of the water,
in the tremulous pulse
of the engine, to lull
the persistent anguish
of old wounds . . .
To drink the sky in winds
that taste of soporific
salts and iodized night air.
Traces of stormy
hopes and longings
dissolve into the mist
like foam into the wave.
—Flowers of softest seafoam
that spring up to either side
of the slicing prow.
Blue of sea and skies . . .
I am nothing and yet now
behold me, finite center
of the infinite sphere
of sea and skies that lie beyond.
—I am where God is.

PILGRIMAGE

Seen from the front, she was an April.
She was an August from the side.
Two women in one: face full in front
but thin in profile.

She shaped her eyebrows like a "˜";
her mouth like an "o" (almost). Having explained this much
I'm not going to say how much I loved her. I don't even like
to recollect—a thousand sorrows!

Eis senão quando um dia . . . Mas, caluda!
Não me vai bem fazer uma canção
Desesperada, como fez Neruda.

Amor total e falho . . . Puro e impuro . . .
Amor de velho adolescente . . . E tão
Sabendo a cinza e a pêssego maduro . . .

ENTREVISTA

Vida que morre e que subsiste
Vária, absurda, sórdida, ávida,
Má!

    Se me indagar um qualquer
Repórter:
    "Que há de mais bonito
No ingrato mundo?"
              Não hesito;
Responderei:
           "De mais bonito
Não sei dizer, Mas de mais triste,
— De mais triste é uma mulher
Grávida. Qualquer mulher grávida."

O BEIJO

Quando a moça lhe estendeu a boca
(A idade da inocência tinha voltado,
Já não havia na árvore maçãs envenenadas),
Ele sentiu, pela primeira vez, que a vida era um dom fácil
De insuputáveis possibilidades.

Except that when one day . . . But enough!
It's not for me to write a song
of despair à la Neruda.

Love perfect and imperfect . . . Pure and impure . . .
Love of an old adolescent . . . And with so strong
a taste of ash and ripened peaches . . .

INTERVIEW

Life that dies and that subsists
fickle, ludicrous, grasping, vile
defiled!

      If some reporter one day
asks me:
      "What is the most lovely thing you find
in this thankless world?"
                  I won't hesitate; I'll
tell him:
                "Most lovely?
I don't know. But saddest by a mile—
the saddest is a woman—
any woman with child."

THE KISS

When the girl offered him her lips
(the age of innocence had dawned anew,
there were no longer poisoned apples on the tree)
he felt for the first time that life was a gift
of infinite possibility.

Ai dele!
Tudo fora pura ilusão daquele beijo.
Tudo tornou a ser cativeiro, inquietação, perplexidade:

— No mundo só havia de verdadeiramente livre aquele beijo.

ANTOLOGIA

A vida
Não vale a pena e a dor de ser vivida.
Os corpos se entendem mas as almas não.
A única coisa a fazer é tocar um tango argentino.

Vou-me embora p'ra Pasárgada!
Aqui eu não sou feliz.
Quero esquecer tudo:
— A dor de ser homem . . .
Este anseio infinito e vão
De possuir o que me possui.

Quero descansar
Humildemente pensando na vida e nas mulheres que amei . . .
Na vida inteira que podia ter sido e que não foi.

Quero descansar.
Morrer.
Morrer de corpo e de alma.
Completamente.
(Todas as manhãs o aeroporto em frente me dá lições de partir.)

Quando a Indesejada das gentes chegar
Encontrará lavrado o campo, a casa limpa,
A mesa posta,
Com cada coisa em seu lugar.

Woe to him!
Everything was sheer illusion engendered by that kiss.
Everything was soon once more fear, doubt, oppression.

—In the whole world the only truly free thing was that kiss.

ANTHOLOGY

Life
isn't worth the trouble and the grief it takes to live.
Bodies understand each other but souls, never.
The only thing to do is strike up an Argentine tango.

I'm heading off to Pasárgada!
Here I don't have what I need.
I want to forget everything:
—the pain of being human . . .
this vain and ceaseless yearning
to possess what possesses me.

I want to rest
humbly to think about life and the women I have loved . . .
about the whole life that could have been and wasn't.

I want to rest.
To die.
To die, body and soul.
Completely.
(Every morning the airport across the way gives me lessons in
    departure.)

When the Uninvited One arrives
she will find the fields well tended, the house clean,
the table set,
and each thing in its right place.

DUAS CANÇÕES DO TEMPO DO BECO
TWO SONGS FROM THE TIME OF THE ALLEY
1966

PRIMEIRA CANÇÃO DO BECO

Teu corpo dúbio, irresoluto
De intersexual disputadíssima,
Teu corpo, magro não, enxuto,
Lavado, esfregado, batido,
Destilado, asséptico, insípido
E perfeitamente inodoro
É o flagelo de minha vida,
Ó esquizóide! ó leptossômica!

Por ele sofro há bem dez anos
(Anos que mais parecem séculos)
Tamanhas atribulações,
Que às vezes viro lobisomem,
E estraçalhado de desejos
Divago como os cães danados
A horas mortas, por becos sórdidos!

Põe paradeiro a este tormento!
Liberta-me do atroz recalque!
Vem ao meu quarto desolado
Por estas sombras de convento,
E propicia aos meus sentidos
Atônitos, horrorizados
A folha-morta, o parafuso,
O trauma, o estupor, o decúbito!

SEGUNDA CANÇÃO DO BECO

Teu corpo moreno
É da cor da praia.
Deve ter o cheiro
Da areia da praia.
Deve ter o cheiro
Que tem ao mormaço
A areia da praia.

FIRST SONG OF THE ALLEY

Your body dubious, irresolute,
hotly contested by both sexes,
your body, not thin, but lean,
washed, scrubbed, beaten,
distilled, aseptic, without taste
and completely without smell
is the torment of my life,
Oh schizoid one! Oh graceful body!

For its sake I've suffered at least ten years
(years that seem more like centuries)
so many tribulations
I am at times a werewolf
and torn by desire
I rove like a mad dog
late at night through sordid alleys!

Stop this suffering!
Free me from this fierce denial!
Come to my lonely room
in these convent shadows
and feed my senses
astonished, horrified,
the leaflike spin, the downward spiral,
the shock, the stupor, the decumbent body!

SECOND SONG OF THE ALLEY

Your dusky body
is the same color as the beach.
It probably smells
like sand.
It probably smells like sand does
in the warm, moist air.

Teu corpo moreno
Deve ter o gosto
De fruta de praia.
Deve ter o travo,
Deve ter a cica
Dos cajus da praia.

Não sei, não sei, mas
Uma coisa me diz
Que o teu corpo magro
Nunca foi feliz.

NU

Quando estás vestida,
Ninguém imagina
Os mundos que escondes
Sob as tuas roupas.

Assim, quando é dia,
Não temos noção
Dos astros que luzem
No profundo céu.

Mas a noite é nua,
E, nua na noite,
Palpitam teus mundos
E os mundos da noite.

Brilham teus joelhos.
Brilha o teu umbigo.
Brilha toda a tua
Lira abdominal.

Your dusky body
probably tastes
like beach fruit.
It probably has the tartness,
it probably has the acrid aftertaste
of the cashew fruit.

I couldn't say, I couldn't say but
something tells me, yes it does
that your body, your thin body
has never known the joy of love.

NAKED

When you are dressed
no one could guess
the worlds you hide
beneath your clothes.

(Likewise, by day
we have no idea
of stars that shine
in the sky's depths.

But the night is naked
and, naked in the night,
your worlds and the worlds
of night throb.

Your knees shine.
Your navel shines.
The whole lyre of your abdomen
shines.

Teus seios exíguos
— Como na rijeza
Do tronco robusto
Dois frutos pequenos —

Brilham.) Ah, teus seios!
Teus duros mamilos!
Teu dorso! Teus flancos!
Ah, tuas espáduas!

Se nua, teus olhos
Ficam nus também;
Teu olhar, mais longo,
Mais lento, mais líquido.

Então, dentro deles,
Bóio, nado, salto,
Baixo num mergulho
Perpendicular.

Baixo até o mais fundo
De teu ser, lá onde
Me sorri tu'alma,
Nua, nua, nua . . .

NATAL 64

A MOUSSY

Ao deitar-me para a dormida,
Desejara maior repouso
Do que adormecer, a não ouso
Desejar o jazer sem vida.

Vida é possibilidade
De sofrimento; quando menos,
Do sofrimento da saudade,
Com os seus vãos apelos e acenos.

Your little breasts
—like two small fruits
on a taut,
firm trunk

shine.) Ah, your breasts!
Your firm nipples!
Your back! Your thighs!
Your shoulders!

If you are naked, your eyes
are naked too;
your gaze slower,
longer, more liquid.

Then, in them
I drift, I swim, I leap,
I descend in a perpendicular
dive.

I descend to the depths
of your being, there where your soul
smiles up at me,
naked, naked, naked . . .

CHRISTMAS '64

FOR MOUSSY

When I lay down to sleep,
I'd wanted greater rest
than slumber yet I didn't dare
to dream the dream of death.

Life is the possibility
of suffering—at the least
the suffering of memory
with its futile pleas.

Mas a não haver outra vida,
Aos que morrem pode a saudade
Dar-lhes, senão a eternidade,
Um prolongamento de vida.

Então por que neste momento
Me sinto tão amargo assim?
E a saudade me é um tal tormento,
Se estás viva dentro de mim?

But if there is no other world
our memories can give
the dead, if not eternity,
a longer life to live.

So why then in this moment
am I bitter as can be?
Why is memory such torment
if you live on in me?

PREPARAÇÃO PARA A MORTE
PREPARATION FOR DEATH
1966

PREPARAÇÃO PARA A MORTE

A vida é um milagre.
Cada flor,
Com sua forma, sua cor, seu aroma,
Cada flor é um milagre.
Cada pássaro,
Com sua plumagem, seu vôo, seu canto,
Cada pássaro é um milagre.
O espaço, infinito,
O espaço é um milagre.
O tempo, infinito,
O tempo é um milagre.
A memória é um milagre.
A consciência é um milagre.
Tudo é milagre.
Tudo, menos a morte.
— Bendita a morte, que é o fim de todos os milagres.

PROGRAMA PARA DEPOIS DE MINHA MORTE

> . . . *esta outra vida de aquém-túmulo.*
> GUIMARÃES ROSA

Depois de morto, quando eu chegar ao outro mundo,
Primeiro quererei beijar meus pais, meus irmãos, meus avôs, meus
                                                    [tios, meus primos.
Depois irei abraçar longamente uns amigos — Vasconcelos, Ovalle,
                                                    [Mário . . .
Gostaria ainda de me avistar com o santo Francisco de Assis.
Mas quem sou eu? Não mereço.
Isto feito, me abismarei na contemplação de Deus e de sua glória,

Esquecido para sempre de todas as delícias, dores, perplexidades
Desta outra vida de aquém-túmulo.

PREPARATION FOR DEATH

Life is a miracle.
Each flower,
with its shape, its color, its fragrance,
each flower is a miracle.
Each bird
with its feathers, its flight, its song,
each bird is a miracle.
Space, infinite,
space is a miracle.
Time, infinite,
time is a miracle.
Memory is a miracle.
Consciousness is a miracle.
Everything is a miracle.
Everything, except death.
—Blessed be death which is the end of all the miracles.

PROGRAM FOR AFTER MY DEATH

" . . . this other life on this side of the tomb."
GUIMARÃES ROSA

After my death, when I reach the other world,
I want first of all to kiss my parents, my brothers and sister,
    my grandparents, aunts and uncles, cousins.
Then I'll give a big hug to some friends—Vasconcelos, Ovalle,
    Mário . . .
And after that I'd like a word with Saint Francis of Assisi.
(Though who am I to ask that? I'm not worthy.)
Once I've done all this I'll lose myself in contemplation of God and
    his glory,
having forgotten for all time the joys, the sorrows, the doubts
of this other life on this side of the tomb.

Notes to Poems

Na Rua do Sabão/Soap Street

The balloon in this poem is not the colored globe of the following poem, "Balões" (Balloons), with which English-speaking readers are familiar, but a homemade paper construction. To rise, these "fire balloons" depended on a burning wick to heat the air within the globe. They are often illegal because of the potential fire hazard.

O Anjo do Guarda/Guardian Angel

Maria Cândida de Souza Bandeira, who had served as her brother's nurse since 1904, died in 1918.

O Cacto/The Cactus

Laocoön was a priest of Apollo who tried to convince his fellow Trojans not to bring the wooden horse left by the Greeks into the city. Angered by his actions, the sea god Poseidon sent two serpents to crush the priest and his two sons. A group of statues commemorating the event is on exhibit in the Vatican Museum.

Count Ugolino della Gherardesca of Pisa (1230–1289) was a Ghibelline who rose to power as leader of the Guelfs. When he betrayed the latter, he and his sons were imprisoned in "the tower of hunger," an event described in Dante's *Inferno*.

Pneumotórax/Pneumothorax

A pneumothorax is a therapeutic measure to collapse a malfunctioning, often tubercular, lung. In the Portuguese version of the poem, the doctor tells the patient, "Diga trinta e três . . . " (Say thirty-three) in order to hear the vibration of the consonantal "tr."

The text is a good example of the *poema-piada* or joke-poem, of which the first generation of Modernists were particularly fond.

Evocação do Recife/Evocation of Recife

Recife is often called "the American Venice" because of the rivers that traverse the city. During the Netherlands' occupation of Northeast Brazil during the first part of the seventeenth century, Recife was renamed Mauritsstad after the Dutch governor, Maurice of Nassau.

The "Portuguese peddlers" were called *mascates* in Portuguese. The War of the Mascates, in which Recife's largely native-born merchants defeated the Portuguese planters of Olinda, occurred in 1710–1711.

"Capiberibe" is the correct pronunciation of one of Recife's principal rivers; "Capibaribe" is the colloquial version. Caxangá, an outlying district of Recife in Bandeira's day, is now a densely populated industrial zone. The English "cavalcade" cannot fully render *cavalhada*, a traditional entertainment still practiced in small towns of the Northeast in which two teams on horseback (Red and Blue, Moors and Christians) attempt to spear a ring suspended in the middle of the street.

Poema Tirado de Uma Notícia de Jornal/Found Poem

Babylon Hill (the "Morro da Babilônia") is one of Rio's infamous *favelas* or hillside shantytowns. As the Portuguese title whose literal translation is "Poem Taken from a Newspaper Article" indicates, Banderia "translated" an everyday journalistic account into poetry.

Oração do Saco de Mangaratiba/Prayer on Mangaratiba Bay

This poem represents a fragment of a much longer text that the poet composed in his head while returning at a very late hour from an excursion. Exhausted, he did not commit the text to paper before falling asleep and, when he awoke, could only remember the lines that appear here.

Mangaratiba, some fifty miles west of Rio de Janeiro, was then a fishing port. Marambaia Island, which is southeast of Mangaratiba, is linked to the mainland by a narrow sandbar.

O Major/The Major

Brazil joined with Uruguay and Argentina to defeat Paraguay in the War of the Triple Alliance (1865–1870). The celebrated battle of the Bridge of Itororó occurred in 1868.

Oração a Teresinha do Menino Jesus/Prayer to Teresinha of Little Lord Jesus

Teresinha do Menino Jesus (literally, "little Teresa of the Child Jesus") is a woman's name borrowed from that of a French holy figure popular in the earlier part of the twentieth century. Such names are particularly common in the Northeast.

Profundamente/In a Sound Sleep

Saint John's Eve, June 22, marks the winter solstice in the Southern Hemisphere. It is celebrated with bonfires and firecrackers to frighten away the evil spirits traditionally believed to roam the earth on this night.

Madrigal Tão Engraçadinho/Such a Funny Little Madrigal

This poem was originally the last line in "Porquinho-da-Índia" (Guinea Pig).

Noturno da Parada Amorim/Nocturne of Amorim Station

The colonel's exclamation, "Je vois des anges!" (I see angels!) intensifies the poem's surrealistic tone. The sobbing at the end of a jingling telephone is reminiscent of a scene that Bandeira describes in "O Místico" (The Mystic) in *Os Reis Vagabundos e mais 50 Crônicas.*

Macumba de Pai Zusé/Voodoo at Pai Zusé's

"Voodoo" would not normally be a good translation for the many-faceted Afro-Brazilian religious sytem known as *macumba*, but this approximation fits the spirit of the poem.

"Pai" means father and is in this case a shortened form of "pai-de-santo" (literally, father-of-the-saint), a macumba priest. "Zusé" is a colloquial form of "José." "Spellbound" ("Encantado") is an outlying district of Rio de Janeiro; Botafogo is located in the center of the city.

Noturno da Rua da Lapa/Lapa Street Nocturne

Lapa is a picturesque red-light district of Rio de Janeiro. The Lenore of the conclusion is a reference to Edgar Allen Poe's "The Raven." The illogic of the last two sentences purposefully intensifies the surreal quality of the poem.

Cabedelo/Cabedelo

Cabedelo (the word in Portuguese for a small sandbank near a river's mouth) is the seaport for João Pessoa, capital of the state of Paraiba. As noted elsewhere, *Journey Around the World in a Nutshell* is a well-known children's story.

Irene no Céu/Irene in Heaven

Irene was one of Bandeira's domestic employees.

Pasárgada/Pasárgada

Bandeira got the idea for this poem at the age of sixteen when he chanced on a reference to "Pasárgada" in a history book. "This name, Pasárgada," he explains, "which means 'field of the Persians' or 'treasure of the Persians,' suggested to me a fabulous landscape, a country of delights like that in 'L'Invitation au Voyage' by Baudelaire (*Itinerário*, 102, my translation).

Mad Joan of Spain (Juana la Loca, 1479–1555), daughter of Ferdinand and Isabel, received this nickname after she began to show signs of mental illness after the birth of her second son. The prolonged absence and numerous infidelities of her much-loved husband, Philip of Austria, aggravated her condition.

Effective birth control measures and direct-dial telephones were not available in Brazil in 1928, the year the poem was written. The Mother-of-Streams (*mãe-d'água* in Portuguese) is a water spirit drawn from Brazilian Indian as well as African folk legends and reinforced by the European idea of the mermaid.

Canção das Duas Índias/Song of the Two Indies

The "Marambaias" to which Bandeira refers are probably an extension in his mind of the Restinga da Marambaia, a sandbar. (See note to "Oração no Saco da Mangaratiba.")

Balada das Três Mulheres do Sabonete Araxá/Ballad of the Three Women on the Araxá Soap Wrapper

The Araxá (pronounced Ah-rah-SHAH) soap wrapper pictured three exotic-looking women. The first part of the second stanza includes a series of references to poems by Olavo Bilac and Castro Alves as well as to a popular Carnival samba by João de Barros, better known as Braguinha. A brancarana is a light-skinned mulatta; an africana, an African woman.

Oração a Nossa Senhora da Boa Morte/Prayer to Our Lady of the Painless Death

The title (literally, "Prayer to Our Lady of the Good Death") is a play on the names of well-known holy figures such as Nosso Senhor da Boa Viagem (Our Lord of the Good Journey) and Nossa Senhora do Bom Parto (Our Lady of the Good Childbirth).

D. Janaína/Dona Janaína

Dona (Lady) Janaína is another name for Iemanjá, goddess of the sea and Afro-Brazilian equivalent of the Virgin Mary.

Rondó dos Cavalinhos/Rondeau of the Little Horses

Alfonso Reyes (1889–1959) was a well-known Mexican writer who served as ambassador to Brazil between 1930 and 1936. The poem, originally titled "Rondó do Jockey-Club" (Rondeau of the Jockey Club) was written for a farewell luncheon in Reyes's honor at this establishment.

The "Esmeralda" of the poem may be a reference to a poem by Augusto Frederico Schmidt which begins "Esmeralda, onde estão teus noivos?" (Esmeralda, where are your sweethearts?) or to the woman of the same name whom Bandeira describes in the short essay "João," in *Os Reis Vagabundos*.

Poema Desentranhado de Uma Prosa de Augusto Frederico Schmidt/ Poem Disentangled from a Prose Piece by Augusto Frederico Schmidt

August Frederico Schmidt was a Brazilian poet (1906–1965) largely concerned with religious themes whose work reveals a decidedly apocalyptic bent. The prose piece "disentangled" here into a poem is Schmidt's description of Bandeira's work.

Desafio/Challenge

Lake Saint Lawrence (o Lago de São Lourenço) in the state of Minas Gerais was a popular resort in Bandeira's time. One of the prime attractions was a lake where boats could be rented.

Canção de Muitas Marias/Song of Many Marias

The poem plays on the heavy use of the name "Maria" followed by one of numerous modifiers such as "das Neves" (of the Snows) or "do Céu" (of the Sky). I have already noted that the Three Marias or Three Marys is a constellation in the Southern Hemisphere and that Bandeira's sister, Maria Cândida de Soua Bandeira, his nurse since 1904, died in 1918.

"Cândida" means "candid" or "pure." Tupi is a Brazilian Indian language. I have translated "Saltei de vara" as "I skipped over a pole"; its literal meaning is to pole vault.

Acalanto de John Talbot/Lullaby for John Talbot

John Talbot was the small grandson of a personal friend.

Poema Só Para Jaime Ovalle/Poem Just for Jaime Ovalle

Jaime Ovalle (1894–1955), a Brazilian composer from Belém who set to music a number of Bandeira's poems.

Escusa/Excuse

Feira de Santa'Ana in the state of Bahia is a gateway to the vast dry backlands region encompassing a large portion of the Brazilian Northeast.

Belo Belo/Lovely Lovely

This is the second of two poems of the same name based on a popular song.

"Vida noves fora zero" (Life's a zero. Nothing matters) refers to a mathematical operation (casting the nines) in which the sum total is always zero.

Poema Para Santa Rosa/Poem for Saint Rose

Raimundo Correia (1860–1911) was a well-known Parnassian poet.

The woman asks, "Será o Benedito?" (Can it really be Benedito?), a reference to the improbable appointment of Benedito Valadares as governor of the state of Minas Gerais by President Getúlio Vargas.

Reposta a Vinícius/Reply to Vinícius

Marcus Vinícius Cruz de Morais (1913–1980) was a poet and lyricist best known for his sonnets and sambas about love.

As Três Marias/The Three Marys

Once again, the poem refers to a constellation in the Southern Hemisphere. The monsters whom the poet mentions are familiar figures in Luso-Brazilian folklore.

Infância/Childhood

The quotation "la fraîcheur des latrines" (the cool freshness of the latrines) is from Rimbaud's poem, "Les poètes de sept ans."

Poema Encontrado por Thiago de Mello no 'Itinerário de Pasárgada'/ Poem Discovered by Thiago de Mello in 'Itinerary of Pasárgada'

Thiago de Mello (1926—), a poet, diplomat, and translator born in Manaus. The poem is taken from a line in Bandeira's autobiographical essay, *Itinerary of Pasárgada*.

Retrato/Portrait

The poem is a description of Bandeira's celebrated fellow poet, Carlos Drummond de Andrade (1902–1987), born in the city of Itabira in the state of Minas Gerais. Longtime friends, the two collaborated in various projects such as *O Rio de Janeiro em Prosa e Verso* (1965).

Consoada/Late Supper

A *consoada* is a light evening meal, often eaten at the end of a religious fast day.

Letra para Heitor dos Prazeres/Lyrics for Heitor dos Prazeres

Heitor dos Prazeres (1898–1966) was a composer of popular music known particularly for his sambas and Carnival music.

Antônia/Antônia

Augusto Meyer (1902–1965), poet, essayist, and critic, was a key figure in the Modernist movement in the southern state of Rio Grande do Sul.

Passeio em São Paulo/A Walk through São Paulo

As noted elsewhere, the quotations in Portuguese within the text are from Mário de Andrade's *Paulicéia Desvairada* (Hallucinated City). Bandeira plays on the traditional Latin phrase Ubi sunt? (Where are they now?) when he demands "Ubi sum?" (Where am I?).

The internationally known painter Emiliano di Cavalcanti (1897–1976) is considered the probable mastermind of the *Semana de Arte Moderna*.

Peregrinação/Pilgrimage

Bandeira is referring to Chilean poet Pablo Neruda's *Veinte poemas de amor y una canción desesperada* (Twenty Love Poems and a Song of Despair).

Antologia/Anthology

A pastiche composed of bits of preceding poems. The initial lines are from the concluding couplet in "Soneto Inglês No. 1" (English Sonnet Number One): "Morrer sem uma lágrima / que a vida / não vale a pena e a dor de ser vivida." All of the other poems utilized in the text appear in this collection.

Primeira Canção do Beco/First Song of the Alley

The "leaflike spin" ("folha morta," literally, dead leaf) in the second-to-last line is a maneuver made by an airplane; the "downward spiral" ("parafuso," literally, screw) is a dance step. Both terms also refer to sexual positions.

Programa para depois de Minha Morte/Program for after My Death

The initial quotation is by João Guimarães Rosa (1908–1967), whom many critics consider to be Brazil's greatest twentieth-century prose writer.

Designer: U.C. Press Staff
Compositor: Janet Sheila Brown
Text: 10 pt. Palatino
Display: Palatino
Printer: Braun-Brumfield, Inc.
Binder: Braun-Brumfield, Inc.